MARC C. DENHEZ

HERITAGE
FIGHTS
BACK

Legal, financial and promotional aspects of Canada's efforts to save its architecture and historic sites.

With an introduction by

PIERRE BERTON

HERITAGE CANADA

I0630597

Fitzhenry & Whiteside
Toronto Montreal Winnipeg Vancouver

A Dedication

Montague, P.E.I.

This book is dedicated to the beautiful community of Montague, Prince Edward Island. That municipality not only forms a valuable part of Canada's heritage, but its city fathers also had the sagacity to enact a municipal by-law making it illegal to heave buildings into the town dump.

© 1978
Published by Heritage Canada and Fitzhenry & Whiteside.

Heritage Canada,
P.O. Box 1867,
Station "B",
Ottawa, Ontario K1P 5R4

Fitzhenry & Whiteside Limited,
150 Lesmill Road,
Don Mills, Ontario M3B 2T5

ISBN 0-88902-563-0

Heritage Canada is a registered charitable organization dedicated to the conservation and promotion of the historic, architectural and natural components of the environment.

Printed and bound in Canada
by Tri-Graphic Printing (Ottawa) Ltd.

Cover: The Père Honorat Mill near Chicoutimi, Que., was derelict until private citizens began restoration; their accomplishment earned an award from Heritage Canada.

CONTENTS

PART III: The Powers That Be

PART IV: The Governments' Financial Techniques

PART V: Spreading The Word

PART VI: Heritage In Action, A Case Study

A NOTE FROM THE AUTHOR

In 1975, an international group of assorted European politicians, intellectuals and others gathered in Helsinki under the auspices of the United Nations Educational, Scientific and Cultural Organization (UNESCO). It was time, they said, for countries to stop moaning about various cultural and environmental problems: they should start trading information about concrete ways to solve these problems. As a direct result, a series of international joint studies was set up.

One of those joint studies was on the subject of protecting sites of architectural and historic interest.

There was only one slightly embarassing problem with the proposed exchanges of information: several delegates to the conference returned home to learn that their country had no information on that subject to exchange. Several joint studies folded in short order.

However, the Europeans who assembled to discuss "heritage sites" were undeterred. If they had no relevant information on hand, then they would find it. They were taken under the obliging wing of UNESCO's European region, and got to work unearthing the legal, financial and promotional explanations of heritage conservation efforts in their respective countries.

Some Europeans, however, have a curious sense of geography. According to UNESCO's map, Canada is in Europe . . . at least for organizational purposes.

Accordingly, Canada was invited to join the European joint studies. The Canadian Commission for UNESCO asked Heritage Canada to do the honours on behalf of Canada. Since a large part of the subject matter covered law and taxation, I was given the assignment.

Naturally, when one assigns a lawyer to write a report, one takes certain risks. First, sentences began with "whereas". Second, the report was three times longer than anyone expected, including myself (but then, that can be blamed as much on the fact that it was written in Ottawa as anything else).

9

A condensed technical version of the report was dutifully sent to the joint study; but meanwhile, colleagues suggested that a text should be produced for the Canadian market ... as long as it did not contain the word "whereas".

Hence this book.

Law is traditionally a boring subject (except to lawyers), and taxation is deadly. I must admit that I had doubts, at first, as to whether the chosen subjects could appeal to anything but a tiny technically-oriented audience; but as my research continued, I was reminded of Will Rogers' phrase: "I don't make jokes; I just watch the government and report the facts." In the area of heritage conservation law, my qualms were dispelled: many laws would bear interest if only for their intrinsic weirdness. Under some statutes, buildings "get lost"; under others, they "go into retirement." In some cases, the law would appear even comical if it did not have such profound social consequences.

This book discusses some of those consequences. Some are decidedly unpleasant, and it may be that there are people who would prefer not to hear about them; one municipal politician said that the next time I showed up in his city, I would leave on a stretcher. Even among "conservationists", there are many who would prefer to believe that Canada's architectural and historic heritage can be protected simply by spreading joy and good will; they feel positively resentful when shown that the subject is legally more complex than that.

Fortunately, these people are in the minority. The majority of analysts of urbanization are realizing that the forces which determine whether buildings stay up or come down are largely "institutionalized", and must be dealt with accordingly

One part of this text, however, caused particularly difficult problems. The European joint study requested that each country submit a "case study" of a heritage area. No such study had ever been done in Canada; but the area which had been the most extensively documented was Vancouver's Gastown. It was therefore the obvious choice; but there were two caveats. First, reports concerning Gastown were frequently contradictory; second, as a benighted easterner, I had never been "over the hump" to the Pacific Coast to see the area first hand.

Fortunately, I was able to obtain some excellent sources on Gastown: Harold Kalman's *Exploring Vancouver,* Liz O'Kieley's *Gastown Revisited,* and Gary Bannerman's *Gastown, the 107 Years,* were extremely useful. Furthermore, three other reports were not only helpful, but I was also permitted to draw upon them for this book: they were the Vancouver Urban Research Group's *Forever Deceiving You* and the Vancouver City Planning Department's *Gastown Economic Study* and *Gastown Visitors' Survey.*

In 1977, I finally had the opportunity of seeing the Gastown area myself, and of discussing it with local experts. People such as Jon Ellis, Nancy Oliver, Liz O'Kieley, Ray McAllister and the executives of the Gastown Merchants Association went above and beyond the call of duty to share information and to express opinions on the area. I am also highly indebted to the *Vancouver Sun,* which provided many excellent pictures of the area and placed its files at my disposal.

The final draft of this manuscript was prepared, over the last few months, with the invaluable advice of Heritage Canada's R.A.J. Phillips, Terry McDougall, Ruth Hornsby and Helen Smith. When the manuscript was finally ready for publication by Heritage Canada the Canadian Commission for UNESCO once again evidenced its continuing support through financial assistance.

In short, this text has been made possible with assistance and participation from many corners, from Helsinki to the Pacific. I am very grateful for that help.

I take sole responsibility, however, for any errors or omissions in this text. Furthermore, the views expressed are mine only; they do not necessarily represent the views of Heritage Canada, of the Canadian Commission for UNESCO, or of any of the other parties mentioned above.

Finally, I must extend my sincere thanks to a truly remarkable Canadian who has honoured me by contributing to this book: Mr. Pierre Berton.

INTRODUCTION

In a little more than a decade, the heritage movement in Canada has advanced from a standing start to a commendable canter. This book tells us how to turn it into a gallop.

It could just as easily be titled *Everything You Need To Know About Heritage But Were Afraid To Ask.* For any individual or organization interested in saving a single building it is an indispensable handbook. But it is more than that: It contains a careful analysis of heritage legislation, as it is and as it ought to be; a history of the heritage movement and a compendium of heritage-oriented organizations; an assessment of the international heritage movement; a record of successes and failures; a précis on building codes; and an examination of heritage criteria to answer that perennial question, "Just what *is* a heritage building anyway?"

Finally, by telling in great detail the full story of one of the great Canadian heritage successes — the resurrection of the Gastown area in Vancouver — this book lays down a battle plan and gives hope to all those community organizations who believe that the word "progress" has very little to do with the wrecker's ball. The story of the Gastown redevelopment, as told here, has all the conflict, tension and drama of a good novel — with a happy ending.

This book has long been needed in Canada. It seems to me that it answers almost every question that has been put to the overworked staff of Heritage Canada since the organization was launched. Anyone who reads it must come to two conclusions; first, that we have in a very short time made unbelievable strides in convincing the public and the politicians of the value of heritage conservation; second, that an appalling task of conversion still lies before us. At least, however, we know where we are headed and in this book, Marc Denhez lays out a blueprint that shows us how we can get there.

Pierre Berton

PART I
THE MOVEMENT

CHAPTER 1

IN THE BEGINNING . . .

GENERAL

On a foggy evening in March 1976 George Galt, who was then Heritage Canada's Research Officer, was hit by a truck. On that evening, all theoretical economic research in heritage matters for a country of over twenty-two million people shut down.

Fortunately, both Canada and George are recovering.

This incident is, however, indicative of an inescapable fact: the "heritage movement" in Canada is still so young and the expertise so thinly spread that it has not yet generated a widespread body of continuing research.

On the other hand, it is a marvel that any expertise has been generated at all. The very existence of the organized movement is remarkable when one understands the forces which were militating against it. Those forces still exist, and will be described later in this book. The fact that the movement has advanced as rapidly as it has over a few short years testifies to the deeply-felt demand for this work on the part of conscientious Canadians, and their determination to donate their own time and resources for the benefit of the public interest.

It is understandable that once a Canadian "conservationist" has seen the proverbial light on the Damascus Road, his next realization is probably of the immensity of the task which still lies ahead.

He must even face disagreement over the word "heritage". Some Canadians argue that it is presumptuous for those of us who are interested in Canada's structural and natural heritage to call ourselves "the heritage movement": they point out (quite rightly) that Canada's heritage is also incorporeal, such as the multifaceted folklore which was brought to this country from a smorgasbord of cultures. However, an understanding of the true meaning of Canada's structural heritage will reveal that our name is well chosen; this topic will be discussed in Chapter 3.

There are some conservationists who, on the other hand, claim no interest in "heritage" whatsoever. They argue that there are other, better reasons to save buildings than architecture, history or aesthetics. They invariably offend the "purists" of the heritage movement (as does everything else) but their co-operation has proved particularly valuable in many instances. A description of their activities is found in Chapter 2.

What is the Canadian heritage movement? The groups mentioned above are hardly the only ones to defy a neat sterotype. Indeed, the movement appears composed of the widest (and sometimes wildest) possible variety of individuals and groups. The way in which dyed-in-the-wool reactionaries and flaming radicals (along with assorted other species) federated together in a significant popular movement is described below.

THE GENESIS OF THE MOVEMENT

There have always been Canadians interested in history. Manitobans had an historical society when their provincial history was barely nine years old, almost before they had any history to study.

Canada's "history buffs" were a long-suffering crew. Few national populations have been as dismally uninterested in their formal history as Canadians . . . possibly because few countries appeared to make as concerted an attempt to make history courses so boring. A country whose textbooks claim that one of its most decisive

16

events was the Pacific Halibut Treaty is in deep trouble.

For decades Canadians lived in a manner generally oblivious to the historical aspects of their surroundings, while the historical societies hermetically discussed the fascinating aspects of Canadian history which were "beneath the dignity" of our schools. It was not a context which lent itself to activism; and even if it had, the laws did not provide any vehicle for activism. If an historic site was threatened, there were occasional pleas for government acquisition; but the most that could usually be hoped for was a pre-demolition photo of the structure for the reference of future generations.

There are some who believe that the turning point came in 1967, when Canada celebrated its Centennial and Canadians relented in their abhorrence of organized patriotism. The Centennial was certainly an excercise in national pride; and national pride can, on occasion, trigger an appreciation of the works of our "forefathers" (including their buildings). It is equally true, however, that innumerable communities chose as their "centennial project" the deliberate destruction of heritage structures in order to replace them with something "more befitting Canada's second century". In that context, "national pride" was as much a liability as an asset.

In some parts of Canada, it is far more likely that the emergence of the movement was triggered by events in (heaven forbid) Washington(!).

During the mid-1960's, a dedicated group of American conservationists succeeded in convincing the U.S. Congress to pass statutes relating to heritage and the natural environment. Oddly enough, it was not the heritage statute which had any short or long term effect on Canadian conservationists; it was the package of environmental statutes. For the first time, conservationists were given effective legal recourses, and activism was thus given an effective vehicle. The small environmental groups acquired legal clout, access to courts, a blaze of publicity and hence mushrooming membership. It is possible that if American legislators had realized the forces they would unleash, they might have reconsidered; but it was too late. As an example, U.S. Supreme Court Justice Douglas invited "the pilleated woodpecker, the coyote and bear, the lemmings as well as the trout in the streams (to) stand before this Court". Environmental awareness swept North America, ready or not, even among people who knew nothing of the legislation which helped make it possible.

In Canada, most of the functions of the environmental groups were co-opted by the government; but despite the absence of effective legal vehicles, "environmental awareness" kept alive a host of small but dedicated environmental groups as well as a sympathetic attitude in the public at large. Conservationists spared no effort to safeguard even the forests and streams which neither they, nor their children, nor their children's children would probably ever see; the environment was deemed worth saving in its own right.

There was only one problem: few Canadians looked at the definition of "environment" in a dictionary. As far as the public consciousness was concerned, "environment" was always somewhere else: parents would pack the children and the dog into the family car on Sunday afternoon to drive off and see some "environment". Many still do.

No one knows how long this schizoid attitude would have continued if the history and architecture buffs had not crawled out of their cherished woodwork and pointed to a simple truth: environment is where we live. If we live in the city, then our city is our environment; we have no streams and forests, but we have streets and roofs and gables and steeples. If bears, moose and beavers have a right to have their environment respected, why don't people?

It is at this point that the heritage movement performed what epistemology calls a "transcendental leap". In other words, it woke up.

At first, in the late sixties, the successes of "environmentalists" (of the pro-nature variety) simply inspired greater confidence among architecture fans, who had also been encouraged by the centennial celebrations. Contact with environmentalists had increased by 1970, and by 1973 a loose coalition began to emerge between the environmentalists on one hand and the history and architecture buffs on the other. It accelerated, and attracted still other people with totally different concerns. People concerned about the destruction of low income housing and "ethnic types" worried about the disappearing character of their neighborhoods joined in the discussions. Communication made it increasingly apparent that these groups had common objectives. It also became unfortunately apparent that they were being plunged into an adversarial context in which nothing but continued and concerted pressure could lead to the achievement of those objectives.

Naturally, the above scenario was not applicable to all Canadian cities. The kind of coalition which was most obvious in places such as Montreal, Quebec City or even Guelph took a rather different form elsewhere. In Vancouver, architecture buffs found themselves in alliance with the Chinese community; in Winnipeg, they associated with local entrepreneurs. In one of Canada's most prominent success stories, that of St. John's Nfld., conservationists mounted their campaign with such speed and efficiency that it was difficult to observe whether any coalitions were being negotiated; if they were, they appeared overtaken by events in that city's remarkable surge of heritage consciousness.

But whether a city's heritage movement is the product of a formal federated structure or that of a single inspired society, the fact remains that below the surface, it still reflects a variety of interests and aspirations, just as the Canadian heritage movement represents a variety of goals.

It is into this fermenting brew that, in 1973, Heritage Canada was plunged ... with what some conservationists interpreted as more noise than splash. A $12,000,000 endowment fund had been deposited in trust for Heritage Canada; to some conservationists, that meant one thing: free money.

It didn't.

Heritage Canada's first annual meeting

Widespread donations by Heritage Canada to groups did not materialize because Heritage Canada was legally foreclosed from making grants. Furthermore, the organization had doubts about investing in isolated buildings when entire *areas* were probably within reach of renovation; but in order to launch renovation on such a scale, careful organization would be required. This is what Heritage Canada undertook immediately. Heritage Canada energetically pursued a positive profile without, however, taking the headline-catching but hazardous shortcut of sit-ins, demonstrations and occupations which characterized some other groups. The organization was, however, using strict adherence to an old proverb as its operating hypothesis: once one has posed the question correctly, one had already found three quarters of the answer.

Accordingly, Heritage Canada launched feasibility studies, entered into negotiations with governments, and started grappling with the major *institutional* problems facing widescale renovation. That does not mean that Heritage Canada sat tight while awaiting the results of its research. On the contrary, it immediately launched a number of programs based largely upon the successful experience of other countries. In other words, work was undertaken for both the short and the long term. Short term results are visible already; and long term results are even now starting to be felt.

THE STATUS QUO

Heritage fans are increasingly thinking about conservation as a system which must reach into all the nooks and crannies of our legal, financial and social structure. Anyone who looks at the "system" today will notice that there are features in it which are decidedly counterproductive. Anyone who feels pessimistic about this situation should, however, heed one bit of advice: he should see what the "system" looked like five years ago.

This book will outline some of the worst features of the "system", both past and present; that may sound like a negative approach, but it is only by indicating the disasters of the past that we can gain some notion of the giant steps which Canada has recently taken and the momentum which this country currently enjoys.

In other words, when surveying the Canadian situation, one may erroneously conclude that any assessment suffers from rampant negativism; but such superficial appearances are unavoidable in an approach which comprises the deliberate identification of problem areas. Now that these problems have been identified and thanks to the early experience already compiled, the heritage movement is in an unparallelled position to propose constructive and realistic solutions.

And that, in little time, is precisely what the heritage movement in Canada intends to do.

CHAPTER 2

HERITAGE AND NOT-SO-HERITAGE

GENERAL

The omnivorous coalition of citizens which constitutes "the heritage movement" is based in part upon individuals who think of Canadian history and aesthetics as so much maple syrup: their real interests are sociology, psychology or economics.

SOCIAL CONCERNS

Heritage conservation is, almost by definition, a "social" concern; but there are differences of degree. Most conservationists are trying to save structures because they are *conducive to an environment* which can be enjoyed by the population; and this goal is particularly important for those members of the population who, because of physical or economic constraints, are not able to leave their environment for more pleasant climes.

Some conservationists go still further. A fair number of supporters of the conservation movement oppose demolition because of its effects upon social dislocation and upon housing.

The dislocating effect of demolition upon neighborhoods is fairly obvious; and the fact that over five thousand housing units are demolished annually in Canada does not help the low-cost housing supply.

If anything is to be done with old housing stock, these conservationists argue that it should be renovated,

The high cost of demolition. In 1967, expropriation for a Winnipeg project led to this eviction

Top and right, the City of Montreal uses renovation as a tool of its low-cost housing program

Below, Toronto's similar Dundas-Sherbourne project

thereby producing good quality housing more cheaply than new public housing, instead of being demolished.

However, the critics of this demolition have also grappled with deeper problems. Demolition usually dislocates that segment of the population least able to cope with it. Furthermore, it tends to reduce supply of the least expensive housing stock in the country, with possible inflationary repercussions which reach through the entire housing market. This problem is the subject of increasing documentation; it has also aroused considerable militancy in that wing of the conservation movement, to the extent that conservationists have even resorted to the occupation of structures in protest against proposed demolition (as in the case of Montreal's St. Norbert Street). That tactic has not been particularly successful, but it has at least attracted public attention to the problem. It was also a somewhat predictable reaction to a severe problem which confronts the collective Canadian conscience.

PSYCHOLOGY

(i) General

One wing of the conservation movement opposes the effect which massive demolition and redevelopment can bear upon public psychology. Its adherents range from sentimentalists to clinical experts.

(ii) The "Sense of Place"

Toward the "sentimental" end of the spectrum are the conservationists who seek to conserve because older buildings evoke a definite nostalgia.

On a more refined level, one finds conservationists who speak of "a sense of place": it is loosely defined as the agglomeration of structures which permit residents to distinguish their environs from others, and thereby identify "home". The loss of this capacity and the accompanying sense of anonymity can allegedly lead to "anomie", "alienation" and an assortment of psychological difficulties which sound as bad as they are in real life.

Above: Anywhere, Canada. Consumers who can afford to leave this environment often turn to older styles (below), even at the risk of artificiality

Research in Canada still has a long way to go before it can fully substantiate this hypothesis, but the task has begun.

(iii) The "Butterbox Backlash"

The opponents of demolition and renovation are sometimes motivated by a reason closely related to the one explained above: these are the conservationists who oppose redevelopment because they dislike the style of architecture which usually accompanies it.

The adherents of this perspective are reinforced by a widespread apathy or antipathy in the Canadian public toward "modern" construction, i.e. Bauhaus derivatives. Although only a few voices in the architectural community are daring to challenge the Gospel According to Gropius, the general public has always enjoyed "butterbox construction" even less than kitsch. Our expensive suburbs are filled with derivatives of traditional styles, (complete with columns that don't support and shutters that don't close) because of the widescale belief that Bauhaus-style homes are deliberately impersonal or (to use a more common expression) "blah".

This 1922 le Corbusier design, similar to the Bauhaus approach, suggests that "modern" architecture is no more "modern" or "progressive" than the Charleston

It does not take undue effort to persuade that same public of the proposition which states that the replacement of traditional decorated structures with "modern" construction is to compound "blahdom".

In the words of a Winnipeg conservationist, "the alienation of buildings by the denial of an architectural heritage can eventually lead to the alienation of humanity, for the character of man is emblazoned upon the works wrought by him"; or, to summarize less poetically, we don't want redevelopment because we don't like it.

Some of the more radical exponents of this view argue that Bauhaus and its derivatives have run their course, are now decadent, and hence deserve to be ignored in comparison with Bauhaus' predecessors. Whether one goes to that point or not, conservationists believe that one can identify with the structures of the past. The public appears to want buildings with which it can identify. Bauhaus and its derivatives are the only schools of architecture in history conceived specifically to deny human identification; consequently, there is an unavoidable backlash which, in part, is voiced through the heritage movement.

(iv) Stress

The argument mentioned above has been carried to even further lengths: some conservationists argue that there is an empirical relationship between "unidentifiable" modern architecture and levels of stress.

This proposition has been difficult to prove. Other conservationists have attempted to establish an empirical link on other grounds: since demolition and redevelopment are almost invariably associated with an increase in population densities, and since such densities can be empirically linked to stress, there is an obvious indirect link between redevelopment and stress. Research on that subject, however, is far from complete, but again the work is beginning.

28

Conservationists question whether man was destined to live like a sardine

ECONOMICS

(i) General

The primary selling point of the conservation movement is economics: it is the economic argument which recruits some of its more powerful allies in business and government, as well as concerned citizenry. The economic aspects of conservation in Canada were first

A recycled interior. Note the emphasis on original materials.

outlined by George Galt in *Investing in the Past,* and more recently in an ever increasing flow of texts and case studies. These aspects are summarized below, and fall broadly into two categories: first, there are the benefits enjoyed by individual owners; second, there are those enjoyed by the public at large.

Some economists with a taste for jargon refer to these aspects as being at the "micro" and "macro" levels respectively.

(ii)The "Micro" Level

As this book will later point out, there is relatively little encouragement given to renovation of heritage structures; instead, there are disincentives. Despite this problem, there is an emerging body of businessmen who are convinced of the profitability of renovation. These entrepreneurs constitute a wing of the heritage movement which maintains the credibility of the movement with the business community in general and which participates in the negotiations to obtain better terms from the financial community.

The objective of these entrepreneurs is frequently to "recycle" buildings. Recycling is not restoration, because it makes no attempt whatsoever to simulate any earlier appearance of the building; nor is it renovation in the traditional sense. Renovation usually implies the removal and replacement of worn-out material; recycling removes this material, but usually attempts to *avoid* replacement. An example of this distinction is mentioned below; but it should first be pointed out that the conservation movement generally approves of this activity only in terms of those structures which do not have sufficient merit to demand restoration: conservationists would be very reluctant to condone the recycling of an outstanding landmark unless the alternative were total demolition. On the other hand, recycling is an ideal method to retain and reinfuse life into ordinary older buildings, and is immensely useful in the particular case of heritage areas where environment is more important than the features of the individual buildings.

Conventional renovation typically replaces worn-out interior walls and ceilings. Costs have sometimes reached $60.00 per square foot, particularly on government projects.

By contrast, recycling will typically strip all covering from brick walls, wooden columns and wooden ceilings, and then leave them exposed (to the maximum extent which insulation and moisture transfer will permit). One fanatic corner-cutter in Winnipeg claims to be recycling at an alleged $1.50 per square foot, which even the most diehard conservationists find hard to swallow.

This technique is designed not only to cut costs, but also for marketing purposes. Visible wood and brick have diappeared from modern office space because of their cost; their presence in recycled buildings adds to marketability, and professional offices are frequently prepared to pay a premium for them.

Naturally, the entrepreneurs engaged in this work seek the preservation of buildings for other reasons than "heritage". They seek structures which are solid, well located, and likely to make money. Some entrepreneurs oppose demolition primarily because it is wasteful and constricts the market of older buldings available for purchase and recycling.

This "vulgar and mercenary" profit motive invariably upsets the purists. It equally invariably impresses many politicians who still believe (as Calvin Coolidge did) that government's "business is business", and who give support accordingly. The profit motive attached to this wing of the movement therefore serves as more of an asset than a liability.

(iii) The "Macro" Level

A wide range of reasons is advanced in support of the proposition that heritage conservation is in the general economic interest of the public.

The effects on municipal taxation are discussed later in this book, and the housing question was mentioned earlier. There are still two further important arguments which underlie the economic thrust of the heritage movement.

The first is the well-known argument concerning tourist expenditure: anyone with a credit card knows how much can get spent in a big hurry in that "quaint little tourist haven". Canada is no exception to the worldwide pattern. According to one national study documented in George Galt's *Investing in the Past,* over 29% of all tourist journeys by Canadians are spent visiting historic and cultural sites: this is the largest single category of Canadian tourist journeys, beating all the fishermen, deer hunters and assorted moosebaggers combined. The economic consequences have been documented in several communities. Indeed, the tourist influx in some heritage areas has become so great that they are now pleading for the establishment of other heritage areas to relieve the pressure.

The other argument relates to waste. The notion of the disposable building, mentioned in the next chapter, is provoking a hostile reaction from citizens who see

Citizens protesting the wasteful demolition of the 30 year old Laurentien Hotel (inset)

resources as finite. This is an awareness which, for obvious reasons, reached Canada later than most other countries.

Exception is taken to the grossly wasteful pratice of destroying magnificent buildings for redevelopment when vacant lots are in abundance. For example, there is currently enough under-utilized land in central Montreal to accommodate the present rate of growth for 120 years, but some three thousand housing units are still demolished annually. This, in itself, is a strong argument used by conservationists.

However, the argument has been carried further. A wing of the conservation movement has asked whether it is not wasteful to demolish any structure when it can still be put to good economic use. One focus of this debate was the Laurentien Hotel in Montreal: its architecture may have been debatable, but conservationists cannot understand why such a large structure should have been demolished when it was less than thirty years old and was still serving a viable and profitable purpose.

The problem of waste inherent in current patterns of demolition and redevelopment appears even more severe when one notes that it is self-generating: waste multiplies waste. The current pattern of fast amortization of construction costs and expected demolition within a generation discourages proper construction and maintenance, thereby accelerating dilapidation. This is again an area which is beginning to enjoy increasing documentation; thoughtful citizens have expressed concern and have accordingly lent their support to the conservation movement.

CONCLUSION

The various individuals and groups mentioned in this chapter are not really fans of "heritage", but are perhaps its best allies: they broaden the base of the movement, and provide information to reinforce the rationale for conservation.

This information can be essential. For decades, conservationists were disregarded as the "goody-goody" Utopians whose aspirations, like motherhood and apple pie, deserved lip service and little more. "Environmental awareness" helped change that picture; but it is unlikely that full co-operation of the governmental and business sectors could ever be secured without the economic information provided by the interests mentioned in this chapter.

Co-operation is, however, a two-way street: the heritage movement sympathizes with many of the aspirations of the people mentioned in this chapter, even though they do not relate strictly to "heritage". Questions such as social justice and the prudent allocation of resources may not always be the prime motivation for the actions of the movement; but they nevertheless demand our serious attention ... if not always as conservationists, then simply as conscientious citizens.

CHAPTER 3

DEFINING THE CANADIAN HERIT-AGE: EXISTENCE, AESTHETICS, ETHOS.

GENERAL

In the Spring of 1976, an international gaggle of conservation experts met in Ladenburg, in the Federal Republic of Germany. In a polite way, Canada's very presence at that meeting was questioned . . . by another Canadian, of course. It is obvious that some people (including Canadians) wonder what, if anything, is worth protecting in Canada.

Canadian conservationists have been faced with that question many times before. In terms of architectural grandeur, Canada has no Versailles, no Vatican, no castles on the Rhine. In terms of date, Canadians see little to compare with Europe's medieval accomplishments, let alone its classical civilizations. Our Viking settlements are a handful of ruins; and the massive pre-Columbian wooden structures of the Iroquois (whose achievement was all the more significant considering the implements at their disposal) have totally disappeared.

It is one thing to say, of course, that Canadians cannot *see* early accomplishments of building on Canadian soil: it is another to say that prehistoric marvels do not exist. The latter proposition would be totally incorrect. The Indians of the plains were erecting symmetrical cairns (called "medicine wheels") for astronomical purposes similar to those of Stonehenge, at a date even earlier than Stonehenge. No one knows how many millenia separate the Inuit builders of landmark cairns (or "inukshuks") from the present day. Earthwork complexes of enormous proportions are sometimes two thousand years old.

It is only within the last fifteen years that archaeology has revealed that the "history of non-residential construction" (if that is what it can be called) in Canada is five thousand years old; the history of construction on a monumental scale is two thousand years old. The difficulty is that most of these works of great antiquity are inaccessible to the general public. Most of the monumental mounds (with some notable exceptions such as Serpent Mound near Peterborough) are deep in the forests; the inukshuks are in the Arctic; and the location of most medicine wheels is concealed by provincial authorities to avert vandalism. Consequently, it is not surprising that many Canadians still labour under the misconception, in line with Hollywood's stereotype of native people, that Canada's prehistory has left us nothing but a quaint collection of arrowheads.

Canada's architectural roots are shrouded in the proverbial mists of time; but the fact remains that Canada still cannot point to an ancient and continuous architectural tradition as many Europeans can do: we would be cheating if we claimed credit for monuments which, only a few years ago, we did not even know existed. When asked "what is the Canadian structural heritage", we must answer that there is no continuous tradition which dates back more than three hundred years; and in most of Canada, that time span is much shorter. In terms of surviving functional buildings, we are left with only a handful of seventeenth century structures in a tiny fraction of the country; and the recentness of the rest is indicated by the criteria adopted by the Canadian Inventory of Historic Building: an "historic" building, according to the Inventory, is generally one built prior to 1914. That standard always succeeds in provoking at least a smile from our European counterparts.

The hill above is no ordinary picnic ground: it covers a 2000 year old ceremonial centre 113 feet in diameter and 24 feet high. However, most native architecture (such as the Iroquois community below) did not survive the European onslaught.

The task of identifying Canada's structural heritage is complicated further. In European nation-states, a relatively homogeneous pattern of cultural development permitted standards of comparison: it is possible to identify a building as representing the best of a *national trend*. The structure could thus be properly called "of national significance".

In Canada, we sometimes refer to buildings "of national architectural significance", but never because the structure epitomizes the achievement of a national indigenous design movement. Until the twentieth century, Canada was too vast and sparsely populated to permit such a movement and hence to provide a common denominator on which comparisons could be based. For example, Quebec and its three neighboring provinces (Ontario, New Brunswick and Newfoundland) developed *at least* four distinct architectural traditions. It is as easy to compare their achievements as it is to compare apples with oranges.

If we nevertheless insist on labelling structures as having national and even *international* significance, it is because we have a different perspective on the definition of heritage.

BASIC ARGUMENTS

General

There are three primary reasons for the protection and revitalization of heritage structures: they are "non-heritage" value (Chapter 2), environmental value, and educational value.

(ii) "Non-Heritage Arguments"

For political purposes, the economic aspect of "non-heritage" value is the most important of all reasons. Most of the decision-makers in our society are relatively unmoved by the other sudsy arguments traditionally made in favour of heritage. Their attitude becomes much more responsive when the financial benefits of tourism, improved municipal finance, and efficient renovation are explained.

Despite the reluctance of some conservationists to touch this "vulgar" and "mercenary" issue, Heritage Canada has been conducting extensive research with the full expectation that the economic argument will be decisive in the future of Canada's structural heritage. Part of that argument, along with other "non-heritage" matters, is to be found in the preceding chapter.

(iii) Environment

The second argument, i.e. the environmental issue, is what attracts the overwhelming majority of Canadian conservationists. This is because many conservationists are first attracted to the *aesthetic* features with which heritage structures endow our communities and land-scapes. Indeed, there is in Canada a small but unduly influential minority of conservationists (the "purists") who believe that aesthetic considerations are the *only* proper criteria for conservation.

The majority of conservationists discount this position, and point to other environmental considerations. Aside from the psychological arguments mentioned in the previous chapter, a more traditional heritage argument has pointed to the desirable features of heritage *areas* whose "aesthetic" characteristics are found in the collective effect of groups of buildings rather than the features of any building taken individually. In that perspective, "scale" and "harmony" have attracted increasing attention.

(iv) Education

The educational argument is the oldest rationale for heritage conservation: it is the argument which was used to justify the world's first conservation statute in Rome in 457 A.D. It seeks the protection of structures because of their capacity to evoke the people or events (historical or otherwise) associated with them. The purists have suggested that there is something deficient in a structure whose only claim to fame is "by association"; on the other hand, some vocal conservationists argue that conserva-

Majorian, the father of heritage legislation, 457 A.D.

tion is irrelevant unless it can teach us something
fundamental *about the society which erected the structure*
in question and thus about the *dynamics of our own
society and of civilization itself.*

(v) "Heritage"

It is the combination of environmental and educational value which is usually defined as "heritage"
value. There are, however, many ways in which an assessment
of that value can be arrived at.

There are almost as many views on the criteria for
labelling heritage as there are conservationists. Consequently, one of the first tasks of any "heritage" planner
has been to adopt a well-systematized methodology for
the identification and ranking of heritage structures. In
the Maritimes, many planners now assign a numerical

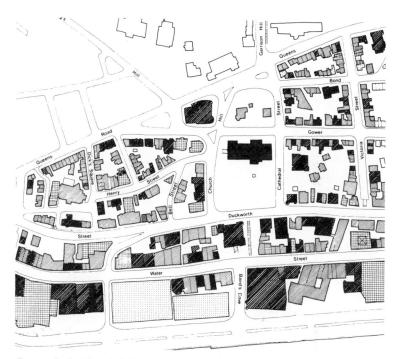

Part of the St. John's coding system as applied to a map of the Newfoundland capital

value to "relative antiquity", "geographic importance", "aesthetic potential", and "environmental quality". These values are then projected on a matrix, ranked according to a relatively sophisticated formula, and then used to colour-code buildings in a proposed heritage area. This mathematical approach invariably impresses decision-makers, sometimes because the latter are so baffled by it that they don't dare criticize.

The criteria mentioned above can, however, be broken down further. Indeed, there is a wide assortment of reasons why structures may be labelled as "heritage". These reasons can be loosely assembled into various forms of categorization. For the purpose of this presentation, that categorization is in three parts entitled existence, aesthetics and ethos.

41

EXISTENCE

(i) General

There are some structures whose very existence is deemed important, regardless of any architectural or aesthetic features. This may be because their existence bears some notable characteristic, e.g. that it is relatively long, that it is attributable to or connected with a special person or event, etc.

The following are examples of these criteria, along with some structures which are associated with them.

(ii) Age

In Canada, with few exceptions (such as the Viking settlement at l'Anse aux Meadows in Newfoundland) the age of a structure must be valued in relation to that of the community. A one hundred year old structure in Quebec is not exceptional; in Alberta, it is mind boggling. In the Northwest Territories, a 1930's building such as the Wildcat Café in Yellowknife can be deemed "historic" without the proverbial batting of an eyelash.

This is because a special value is attached to *the first* structures to be built in a given community. The prairies of Saskatchewan, which cover a larger area than the entire Federal Republic of Germany, were settled within living memory; consequently, the structures of the very first "sodbusters" are occasionally occupied by the retired pioneers themselves. Labelling such structures as "historic" confuses some critics; but since the very act of settlement is probably the most decisive historic event of a community, the structures necessarily acquire an "historic" character regardless of the date of construction.

(iii) Association with an Historic Figure

It is frequent practice to pay special attention to structures which are linked to a prominent historical personality. For example, the residents of Kingston have taken great pains to protect the homes of Canada's first Prime Minister (although St. Catharine's has still done nothing for the home of the immortal Gideon Sundback,

Above, the fort on Ile Ste-Helene, site of de Bougainville's would-be last stand. Instead he reached Tahiti (below), but unfortunately lacked the foresight to annex it to the Montreal Urban Community

inventor of the zipper).

Another memorable site is the fort on Ile Ste-Hélène, facing Montreal. A young French officer proposed to make it his last suicidal stand against the British Conquest in 1760; but Canadians made the futility of this gesture clear to the officer named de Bougainville, who sailed off in a huff for sunnier climes. (Doesn't that make Canadians responsible for the discovery of Tahiti?)

Birth of a Notion: Charlottetown's Province House, where Sir John A. Macdonald and the other Fathers of Confederation first met

(iv) Association with an Historical Event

Certain buildings are notable because of the events which occurred there. For example, the preservation of the Windmill near Prescott, Ontario, is justified simply because it was the focus of a major battle in the rebellions of 1837-8.

Province House in Charlottetown, where Sir John A. signed the guest book as "cabinet-maker" would deserve attention if only because of the weird idea that emerged from a certain conference held there in 1864.

(v) Association with a Scientific, Technological or other such Event

Some sites are protected because of their scientific interest. Aside from archaeological sites (which bear

44

Historic Tar: Bitumount, Alberta

anthropological as well as historic significance) and palaeontological sites, there are other kinds of sites which demonstrate technological accomplishments.

For example, the Government of Alberta has protected the oil extraction complex at Bitumount, Alberta; it was the first plant to undertake the gargantuan task of separating sand from the world's largest oil supply, and operated between 1934 and 1953. (The Alberta Government also hopes that such extraction will revolutionize energy supplies, which would make Bitumount the first designation on record of a *potential* historic site).

The community of St. Paul, Alberta, has attempted to enter this category by building a flying saucer reception centre, but its proposed guests have failed to fulfill this historic aspiration . . . so far.

(vi) Existence as a Functional Component of Past Lifestyles

Awareness of the "history of our forefathers" implies not only a knowledge of historical events, but also a feeling for their entire way of life. This has led to a keen interest in the structures which played a determining part in that lifestyle.

In Ontario, for example, efforts are being made to renovate or restore the small mills which anchored the economic life of early communities. The Maritime provinces would not feel the same without their lighthouses.

In their own way, these structures epitomize the societies which produced them

Changing technology (with some railway encouragement) is casting doubt upon the future of the grain elevators or "prairie schooners" which have symbolized life in the west. These various structures are now being valued as the representation of the entire economic existence of past generations.

(vii) Existence as a Not-So-Functional Component of past Lifestyles

As opposed to those structures which embody a view (and even some occasional nostalgia) toward the sterling aspects of past lifestyles, there are those which are testimony to the opposite kind of behaviour (!)

Laurier House in Ottawa, Ontario, displays the room where Mackenzie King, Canada's Prime Minister of twenty-one years, held séances whereby the dearly departed advised him how to run the country.

The less palatable side of past behaviour is also revealing. One of the examples is "the Hole" in Fredericton, i.e. a pit dug under the old guardhouse in which to throw prisoners who became too unpleasant.

On the brighter side, the Department of Indian Affairs and Northern Development is conducting work on a (highly representative) bordello in the gold rush city of Dawson (we are informed, however, that no restoration would be operational).

Sentries still stand guard at Fredericton's Guard House, site of "the Hole"

(viii) **Existence Attributable to Unusual Circumstances**

Occasionally, a structure came into existence as the result of revealing circumstances, and this reason can be advanced in support of its preservation.

The Canadian Parliament Buildings stood on Montreal's Place Viger until a radical reactionary mob burnt them to the ground in 1848. In memory, the site was left as an empty space to this day . . . except for one particularly appropriate construction: Montreal's first firehall.

The top of Manitoba's Legislative Building owes its appearance to the customs of a different time. The Manitoba government ordered a very expensive statue from France which, after many delays (including a World War), arrived in Winnipeg. When the long-awaited statue named Golden Boy was unveiled in Winnipeg, it was noticed that (gasp!) Golden Boy had no clothes(!). In response to the assorted shrieks and howls, the government decided to use Golden Boy to adorn the pinnacle of the Legislature Building . . . at a sufficiently discreet distance to protect public morals.

They were not amused: Golden Boy had a boisterous trip to the top of the Manitoba Legislature

(ix) Unusual Construction Techniques

Some structures deserve attention because of the uniqueness or ingenuity of the methods by which they came into existence.

For example, no one who saw the façade of the Empire Hotel in Winnipeg could possibly guess that it was built of a cast zinc alloy.

The world's longest cantilever bridge at Quebec had its central span hoisted hundreds of feet from the St. Lawrence River below. At the turn of the century, it was called "the eighth wonder of the world"; but construction took seventeen years and eighty-eight lives.

AESTHETICS

(i) Taste

There are some structures which have acquired a reputation for architectural excellence, and which de- *Not* serve protection accordingly. *taste!*

They require little explanation: they speak for themselves, as does the Lieutenant Governor's Residence in

Lieutenant Governor's residence, Charlottetown.

Charlottetown, or the Greenock Presbyterian Church in St. Andrew's, New Brunswick.

In other cases, a building may contain meritorious components even if the total result is unexceptional. For example, the Quebec Minister of Cultural Affairs did not consider the Quinlan Building in Westmount sufficiently important to protect the entire structure: instead, its noteworthy portals were singled out for protection. Such attempts have not encountered great success.

(ii) A Master Builder

Even when a structure does not represent the height of the accomplishment of a famous architect or builder, it still bears interest. It bears even greater interest when it is a fine example of his work.

Such, for example, is the case of the humble (or not-so-humble) gas station by the world-famous Mies van der Rohe at Ile des Soeurs, Quebec. Similarly, Montreal's Mount Royal Club was designed by Stanford White whose fame, fun and frolic were not confined to architecture . . . until he was gunned down by an irate husband.

(iii) Craftsmanship

Some buildings should be preserved in recognition of the extraordinary craftmanship with which they were built.

For example, the carpentry in the Anglican Church at Moose Factory Island in Ontario was so carefully done that the building is watertight; so there was real consternation when the Moose River flooded . . .

When the church was towed back, holes were drilled in the floor to prevent it from floating away again.

(iv) Decorative Extravaganzas

There were owners and builders who believed, like Oscar Wilde, that "nothing succeeds like excess". Some structures, such as the Bank of Montreal building and Notre Dame Church in Montreal, and the British Columbia Legislature in Victoria did not overstep the boundary of architectural bombast. Others, such as Casa

Everything-including-the-kitchen-sink: above, Casa Loma; below, Chateau Dufresne

Loma in Toronto and the unbelievable Chateau Dufresne in Montreal have raised the eyebrows of aesthetic purists (even when they were built) but retain an endless ability to fascinate.

Architecture as a religious statement: church in Krydor, Saskatchewan

(v) Ethnicity

The peoples who settled Canada brought many architectural traditions with them, and frequently used architecture as an assertion of identity.

These assertions can be as solemn as the byzantine style of Orthodox churches, or as eccentric as the temple of a homesick Greek in Vancouver. In either case, (and despite the occasional cries of "kitsch!") they contribute needed variety and interest to our communities, as well as a taste of the culture they represent.

(vi) Harmony

On occasion, an individual structure without any special inherent characteristics may be as essential to the value of the streetscape as an individual column or pediment is to the value of a building. It consequently deserves protection.

Such is particularly the case in "heritage areas". Excellent examples can be found not only in picturesque places like St. John's and Winnipeg, but also in hundreds of other communities large and small. Officials sometimes have great difficulty in visualizing how otherwise standard buildings can become highly attractive in the context of an area conservation program. However, examples, such as the Ottawa market area and Vancouver's Gastown have demonstrated the potential which exists even among relatively unassuming buildings.

Rhythm and continuity: the architecture of St. John's

Sharon Temple, Sharon, Ontario

(vii) Unusual Architecture

As opposed to styles which epitomize general tendencies, there are those which are totally unusual.

The Sharon Temple in Sharon, Ontario, is a unique building which testifies to the uniqueness of its builders, a defunct sect of musical Quakers

A much more recent addition to Canadian architecture was Buckminster Fuller's ingenious geodesic dome in Montreal, although any good northerner may insist that Mr. Fullers contraption "plagiarizes" their *DEW* line Radar Domes.

Buckminster Fuller's big bubble

(viii) Regional Architecture

Increasing attention is being paid to the styles of construction which can be directly associated with the identity of regional inhabitants and which have the capacity to evoke a feeling for our forefathers and their lifestyle.

The Maritime Provinces developed a number of different architectural styles

Quebec and Ontario developed their own architectural styles. A distinctive character can also be found in prairie communities such as Arcola Sask. (bottom), site of the movie version of "Who Has Seen The Wind."

At the turn of the century, British Columbia mass produced buildings such as this bank in Creston. Above, a train load of prefabricated banks leaves Vancouver

ETHOS

(i) Individual Initiative

Some structures represent significant examples of a person's individual effort. That effort may have been motivated by a wide variety of reasons, from altruism to personal profit; but the result is still noteworthy.

One example is the tinsmith's house in Ottawa. The local tinsmith made the entire facade of the house himself (out of tin, obviously).

An even more individualistic example is the structure built by a British Columbia eccentric in the Kootenay Mountains: it is built with bottles of embalming fluid.

The Sam Kee Building in Vancouver's Chinatown is yet another example. Street construction had left Sam Kee with a narrow strip of land which he offered to sell to either the city or his neighbors. The ridiculously low offers only succeeded in thoroughly angering him. Undeterred, he proceeded to build the world's narrowest building, one block long and 4 ft. 11 inches deep.

(ii) Collective Initiative

The collective initiative which certain structures represent can best be understood by some examples.

The City Hall in Kingston, Ontario, is noteworthy for a number of reasons. It possesses many interesting architectural features, and was designed by an important Canadian architect, George Brown.

The most important feature of this enormous and magnificent structure, however, is rarely mentioned: it was built by a community of barely six thousand people, in a land which was still in the process of initial settlement.

Kingston City Hall

The Anglican cathedral in Fredericton is another structure whose architecture is very pleasing. Again, its most remarkable feature is largely ignored. In the 1840's, this lumbering community in the forests of New Brunswick undertook to build what they thought was the first cathedral on British soil since the Reformation, and to dig the first British cathedral foundations since the Norman Conquest. Since an Anglican cathedral could not legally be located in a village, a special decree had to be passed changing Fredericton's legal status: the community had less than five thousand inhabitants.

Fredericton's Christ Church Cathedral. Although its claim to being the first Anglican cathedral built from scratch since the Reformation is contested by Quebec City, it remains an impressive accomplishment.

In the coastal forests of British Columbia, the inadequacy of implements had limited native production of large works of art; but the arrival of metal tools seemed to release an explosion of pent-up creativity. The "totems" and building decorations consciously depicted family pride and particularly achievements of cunning (British Columbia tribes being among the few cultures in the world to believe that outwitting opponents was more prestigeous than defeating them). These peoples developed a nucleus of artistic tradition into some of the world's greatest and largest masterpieces of design . . . within a single generation.

The town of Canmore, Alberta, "emerged" in the 1880's when coal was discovered. The miners who settled this rough community decided to build the most improbable of all structures: an opera house.

The community of Skedans, British Columbia, as it appeared in 1878. Note the size of the man in the doorway at left

Since they only had logs to work with, the end result looked decidedly different from the masterpieces of Europe; but that did not keep sopranos such as Dame Nellie Melba from marvelling at the acoustics.

Stanley Mission in northern Saskatchewan is a large church built in the 1850's. Every item except the lumber had to be shipped piece by piece from England through the arctic ice and down through Hudson Bay to Churchill, Manitoba. There the parts (including large stained glass windows) were unloaded onto large rowboats, and rowed up the Churchill River for a distance of some nine hundred miles to its present site, where it was reassembled. The structure, many thousands of miles from England, is still accessible only by canoe.

Stanley Mission, Saskatchewan

This is the heritage of Canada

Until now, this text has referred to Canada's "structural heritage"; but that qualifier can be dropped. These structures symbolize so much of what made this country what it is: to understand them is to understand much of what is Canada.

As a general rule, the Canadian environment is not hospitable. It is estimated that only seven percent of its land mass is conducive to agricultural settlement; that represents less than the amount of territory which is permanently frozen. Ottawa is the world's coldest national capital (average temperature in Moscow is higher). Virtually half of the country sits on the Canadian shield, the world's oldest and largest expanse of solid rock.

It is with this environment that our native peoples learned to cope, and to which millions of immigrants migrated. They were short of tools, short of craftsmanship, short of resources, and short of money; and yet, out of either necessity or compulsion, they had the desire to make their mark upon the land. The three most important events in Canadian history were settlement, settlement and settlement. Its structures are its testimony; its buildings are its heritage, to a degree which perhaps surpasses that of any other country in the Western world.

The structural heritage of Canada is an act of will: from the dirt floor of the pioneer's cottage to the steeple of Stanley Mission, from the religious passion which imbues Montreal's Notre Dame to the capitalist ostentation

Some pioneers wondered whether spring was much of an improvement over a Canadian winter

of Toronto's Casa Loma, these structures were first and foremost a conscious assertion of presence.

It is in this sense that Canada's structural heritage is both different from and similar to that of other countries.

It is different in the following way. Our structural heritage was built under conditions generally unknown in Europe since the Middle Ages, and sometimes unique. In terms of human accomplishment, it bears a significance which perhaps surpasses that of many palaces and baroque churches: for the last five hundred years, the heritage of Europe has been the projection of circumstance, whereas, the heritage of Canada has been the defiance of circumstance.

On the other hand, Canada's structural heritage shares the identifying features of the heritage of all civilized countries. The accomplishments of a civilization possess, in Kenneth Clark's phrase, "a sense of permanence". "Civilized man", said Clark, "must feel that he belongs somewhere in space and time; that he consciously looks forward and looks back". The word "heritage" itself implies an achievement which its creators could be proud of and hence could transmit to future generations. It is this sense of achievement which is the common link in the heritage of all countries. The components of heritage may differ from place to place but their meaning and importance are universal.

CONSERVATION IN CONTEXT

It is ironic that the very features which helped make Canada's heritage significant are now threatening its existence and forcing us to rethink the meaning of our society.

The relatively small area of inhabitable territory has led to staggering differences in population density. For example, by the 1990's the ribbon of land in southern Quebec and Ontario will need to support over nineteen million people. This growth is almost entirely urban: since World War II, Canada has enjoyed (or suffered) the highest rate of urbanization in the Western world, and although our ten major metropolitan centres comprise less than 45% of the population, they absorb over 60% of national growth. In southern Ontario alone, one recent estimate suggested that prime farmland was disappearing at the rate of 27 acres every hour.

The myth of the typical Canadian as singing Mountie or mad trapper is long gone: the average Canadian is irretrievably urban. The definition of a Canadian as someone who can make love in a canoe has faded into wishful thinking. The day is fast approaching when the typical inhabitant of the world's second largest country will not exist in green surroundings until after he is dead.

Since our metropolitan areas usually correspond to the oldest settled areas, the toll on our heritage has been devastating. Of approximately 200,000 structures on the Canadian Inventory of Historic Building, a disproportionately low number, 30,000, remain in the nine largest metropolitan centres. Among residential structures alone over five thousand housing units are demolished annually.

The galloping growth of our urban centres has also affected heritage beyond their boundaries. Their economic growth has attracted population away from the countryside, and in some areas (particularly on the prairies) rural depopulation has led to the disappearance of entire communities.

We have never reached a state of equilibrium with the land: in some parts of the country, we have not only conquered nature, we have tried to clobber it into submission; in other parts, mankind gave up in defeat. Dawson, in the Yukon, was once a city of forty thousand; it now has five hundred inhabitants, and the forest is ever so slowly reclaiming its territory. Can a country like Canada ever reach a balance? The question is open for debate.

This phenomenon underscores two contradictory tendencies in the Canadian ethos. The reality of the Canadian environment presented a worthy challenge to

Canadians have sometimes tried to clobber nature into submission . . .
and sometimes given up in defeat

those who wished to establish a lasting presence, but among others it bred a parasitic mentality which sought only to exploit the land and then abandon it.

The lack of commitment still exists. Untold numbers of Canadians lie awake nights dreaming of shuffleboard in Florida. Admittedly, winter in Edmonton or Montreal can be described only as a mixed blessing at best; and yet Canada would not have grown as it has if the country did not offer a good life, in so many respects, to its present inhabitants and to generations to come.

That is what makes current patterns so disturbing: for the attitude of "take the money and run" seems to be increasing, rather than decreasing. Nowhere is this more noticeable than in real estate development. A committee of the Canadian Standards Association is studying a recommendation to put new building blueprints on microfilm for the wreckers who will need to refer to them *"in thirty years"*.

We have entered the age of disposable architecture. What comes next: disposable art? disposable culture? disposable civilization?

Where is the "sense of permanence" which is essential to cultural survival? Has life in the shadow of The Bomb made us so paranoid that subsconsciously we no longer dare to attempt creations of lasting value? Or is it because we have become cynical about "lasting values"? Whatever the answer, it would be a sad day indeed if the only members of society who dared to look forward thirty years were in its wrecking industry.

This is why the heritage movement is so important on a broader level. There are, of course, the aesthetic purists and museum fans who view the movement only as an instrument to preserve "pretty" buildings and "quaint" anachronisms; but the roots of the movement are much deeper. The heritage movement stands for the principle that man has consciously attempted to bring lasting improvements to his environment. A society which is not capable of appreciating that effort is not capable of understanding the meaning of initiative and creativity

66

in particular, and lasting values in general. Such a society is consequently not likely to produce any lasting achievement of its own.

That is the basis on which the first heritage statute was passed by Majorian in Rome in 457 A.D. It was hoped that the heritage of the past would serve as an inspiration for the accomplishments of the future. Instead, Majorian was assassinated, his reforms suppressed and, in Gibbon's words, "the degenerate Romans, who converted the spoil to their own emolument, demolished with sacrilegious hands the labours of their ancestors". Majorian was, however, vindicated in one crucial respect: history proved that he was indeed correct in treating disregard for heritage as symptomatic of general culture stagnation. Within fifteen years of his death, the Empire in the West had collapsed.

Historical parallels are, of course, too simplistic. It is unlikely that our society is on the verge of collapse; it rests too heavily upon technology, which is continuing to evolve. But what about our culture? Where is it going? For that matter, does anybody really know where our culture has been going over the last forty years?

Like all other products in the consumer society, it has become mass producible, mass usable, mass disposible. It suffers primarily from an overdose of transience. Although change is an indispensable ingredient of our society, the word "progress" implies change of *lasting* value; otherwise, change will simply be a superficial disguise for fundamental stagnation and ultimate decadence.

An understanding of this paradox lies at the very basis of the heritage movement. In its most basic sense, the heritage movement seeks to guarantee that our society will choose not to destroy the past, but to improve upon it.

It is the duty of the heritage movement to transmit this consciousness to society as a whole. As Majorian pointed out, the subject is more than "heritage": it is the direction of civilization itself.

PART II
LEGAL TECHNIQUES

CHAPTER 4

HERITAGE LAW IN GENERAL

INTRODUCTION

Anyone who tries getting answers from government learns at least one thing: Canada has a complex bureaucracy. Canada's fundamental constitutional document, the *British North America Act, 1867* (as amended), grants *exclusive* jurisdiction in certain subjects to either the federal government or the provinces. In certain topics an overlap is inevitable, and this overlap creates difficult constitutional problems. Heritage conservation occasionally is an example.

To further complicate matters, provinces delegate some of their powers to subsidiary levels of government, i.e. municipalities. These levels of government are organized as cities, towns, villages, townships, counties, or other "creatures of the legislature" as one New Brunswick judge cryptically called them. In addition, a fourth level of government standing between the municipalities and the provincial legislatures has been created in districts where a partial fusion of municipalities has taken place. This level is called a regional community, urban community or other such "creature".

Jurisdictional disputes can become delightful; and some argue that they are Canada's favorite spectator sport. Conservationists sometimes get confused. There is no doubt that these various levels of officialdom all have felt sympathy for heritage conservation; when historic

68

structures were threatened, many officials were concerned (though not really upset); when the structure tumbled, they were also concerned (though not upset); but when a structure was saved by some *other* official, *then* many became upset.

There are no easy solutions to this problem: it will be endemic to the Canadian system of government for the foreseeable future. There is, however, a way to alleviate the problem: it is to increase the awareness of heritage on the part of *all* governmental levels, to translate that awareness into legal and moral *obligations,* and thereby impose an imperative need for co-operation which does not currently exist. Although most of Canada has stopped short of imposing such a legal obligation on its officials, the level of official awareness and sensitivity has unquestionably increased. In a straw poll conducted five years ago, Heritage Canada learned that many officials at that time did not even know what "heritage" meant; a comparison with governmental policies today is necessarily encouraging. Whether this awareness will be translated into statutes remains to be seen.

However, before we can speculate about the future of heritage legislation, there must be some grasp of the extent of rights and obligations concerning heritage under existing laws.

FEDERAL ACTIVITY IN HERITAGE MATTERS

The Federal Government has been dabbling in the conservation game ever since it created Banff National Park in 1887. This move protected a cavernous basin of sulphur springs intended to satisfy spa-lovers' taste for smelly water. From these inauspicious and definitely unaromatic beginnings, federal government activities grew and grew, and eventually seeped into the subject of "Historic Conservation". The 1952-53 session of parliament gave its seal of approval by enacting the *Historic Sites and Monuments Act* at the same time that it re-enacted the *National Parks Act*.

69

The smell of rotten eggs attracted explorers to this underground basin in the home of Canada's national conservation system

There are, however, a few unavoidable snags in this federal legislation. Constitutionally, all matters pertaining primarily to "property and civil rights" are of exclusive *provincial* jurisdiction. Therefore, although the federal government goes through the exercise of naming "national historic sites", it cannot protect the properties so named and such designations have no legal effect.

Successive federal Ministers of Indian Affairs and Northern Development nevertheless named some 700 "national historic sites". One such site was demolished within days of being named; the site is now occupied by a row of stores and a large parking lot.

The federal government can, however, purchase historic sites. Over one hundred historic sites have been acquired by the government, and are being scrupulously restored. The restoration of one site alone has cost over twenty million dollars. The overwhelming majority of such sites are now being used as museums.

Left, Rideau Street Convent, Ottawa; within days after the Minister declared his intention of naming it a "national historic site", it became a parking lot (right)

(i) Procedures

In matters pertaining to historic sites, the Minister consults an advisory body called the Historic Sites and Monuments Board of Canada. When a structure is brought to the attention of the Board, it first screens applications which are beyond its terms of reference (e.g. cemeteries) and, after study, makes a recommendation to the Minister. The study period is usually some six months long.

The Board may recommend that the Minister a) ignore the structure, b) designate the structure as a national historic site and erect a plaque, c) enter into a *cost-sharing* agreement, or d) acquire the property. The Minister is not bound by that recommendation.

(ii) The Role of Heritage in National Policy

There is no shortage of federal agencies which affect heritage: a 1976 federal publication listed some forty-five different agencies. On the other hand, despite this mass of governmental endeavour (or perhaps because of it), this same publication stated that "there is no federal policy affecting heritage".

That was July, 1976. In order to appreciate the dimensions of the upheaval which occurred in the following two years, it is necessary to look at the factors which led to the civil servants' grim appraisal in 1976.

Some conservationists had been asking whether the federal government was destroying heritage by accident or whether it was making a special effort. One government project was already flattening half of Montreal's colourful Chinatown, and the very department responsible for historic conservation efforts destroyed the Pacific coast studio of Arthur Lismer, one of the greatest painters in Canadian history.

Something had been getting unstuck.

The conservationists most sensitive to these problems were those in the federal government itself. Ottawa had, after all, taken the trouble to recruit some of the best experts in the country to work on heritage matters; they were among the first to realize that the federal government had to be protected from itself. After strenuous efforts, their work paid off.

Half of Montreal's colourful Chinatown was demolished for a federal office complex; such problems led to a major shift in federal policy

The federal government created a body with the unwieldy title of Federal Advisory & Co-ordinating Committee on Heritage Conservation, or FACCHC (rhymes with "match"?). Some pundits groaned "Oh no! not another study committee!"

But they hadn't seen anything yet. There are committees, and then there are *committees*.

Despite the dictum that the functions of officials vary in inverse proportion to the length of their titles, the federal government loaded the FACCHC with one of the most influential and cerebral groups of civil servants in Ottawa. Indeed, it is interesting and characteristically Canadian to note that the achievements of these Canadians was sometimes better known outside Canada than domestically. An official could disregard the opinion of such people only at his peril.

It is this group which was given the responsibility of assuring that federal projects and programs respected heritage; although it has preferred to keep a surprisingly low profile, not even the worst cynic has been able to question its effectiveness in putting the government on the right track.

In other words, the direction of the entire federal government appears to have been altered within less than two years, with almost no outward appearance of flap or ruckus.

It follows that many cases of federal destruction of heritage can now be averted if the problem can be brought to the FACCHC's attention — usually via the Department of Indian Affairs and Northern Development.

A COMPARISON

This entire method of dealing with heritage problems through quiet interdepartmental diplomacy is radically different from the approach of some other countries, where national policy has been translated into legislation and then heaved into the judicial system.

An old American proverb postulates that in order to

teach something to a mule, one must first hit it over the head with a two by four in order to attract its attention; our neighbours to the south have applied the same principle to their officials, presumably on the assumption that bureaucrats and mules are of related species. In terms of heritage, this hypothesis has led the Americans to stack their legislation with provisions *forcing* officials to take heritage into account whenever public works or expenditures were being planned; otherwise, they get clobbered with lawsuits.

As early as the 1960's, the American government enacted sweeping legislation (such as the *National Environment Policy Act* and particularly the *Urban Mass Transportation Assistance Act*) to commit itself to the protection of its own heritage. Australia followed with similar legislation. These statutes insist that any project with federal participation must avoid destruction of historic and architectural heritage unless no viable alternative is possible. At any given time, there are some twenty applications for injunctions pending before American courts to block projects which allegedly harm the cultural and natural environment.

Although the new laws did not provoke a deluge of litigation, they led to some important judicial decisions which both saved valuable heritage and instilled a more conscientious attitude in government planners regarding historic and architectural heritage.

Conservationists are conducting legislative research based in part upon the *Urban Mass Transportation Assistance Act* and related legislation. The unusual feature of these foreign statutes is that the protection of cultural property is no longer contingent upon inventories of heritage.

Inventories of protected buildings had always been considered a *necessary evil* in heritage legislation. They were necessary because a clear distinction was considered essential between indispensible national heritage and *expendable* property. The drafting of inventories was considered an "evil" for four reasons:

74

a) It was subject to lobbying.

b) It placed government in a conflict of interest when the government which was drafting the inventory was also proposing to demolish the structure.

c) It was a never-ending process; for example, the Swedes have not completed their inventory, although they started it in 1666.

d) It tacitly stygmatised properties which were not, for any reason, on the inventory.

The American statutes took a different tack. They said that whenever the federal government proposed to discombobulate an area for a public works project, it would have the obligation to assess the impact of its own actions. If potentially valuable historic architectural sites (on an inventory or not) would be lost, then the government would have to prove that no reasonable alternative existed. If, according to expert testimony, the government had underestimated the heritage value of these properties, then any citizen could apply for an injunction to stop the project. The use of inventories became largely academic.

The reasoning behind the statutes is fairly clear. Governments should not, in conscience, go around wrecking the national heritage if they can possibly avoid it.

When is a place a heritage site? Two groups of people are presumed to know. First, there is the owner himself; proprietors are generally assumed to know something about their property. Second, experts may well have knowledge of the property; their knowledge and their credibility will vary according to their qualifications. If a governmental project threatens a site, and if the balance of evidence indicates the site can legitimately be called an important part of the citizenry's heritage, then the project will be halted by the American courts as being antisocial; no tears will be shed for the frustrated bureaucrats, for they should have known better.

The courts have applied the statutes in an orderly fashion, and no undue problems have disrupted the judicial or administrative system.

Furthermore, the statutes extended to other areas: they prohibited the government from *subsidizing* any project which wantonly harmed heritage. Since most federally-regulated enterprises (such as railways) receive some kind of subsidies, the statutes also affected their activities.

Which system is more effective? The Americans may claim that their system is less "bureaucratic" and more "democratic" since it invests more power in the citizenry. The Canadians can reply, with justification, that it is the result that counts, and we can have no complaint with the FACCHC.

The question remains, however, as to how long the FACCHC can maintain its current level of performance. Increasing demands made upon it will necessarily raise its profile; will that harm its current ability to work behind the scenes in dissuading federal officials from undertaking damaging projects? Will an increasing workload take its toll upon the members of the FACCHC who already have other responsibilities as well?

These questions are more than academic. The FACCHC has yet to sink its teeth into the complicated issue of *federally-regulated works,* i.e. property which is supervised by the federal government but privately owned. Such property includes railway stations, harbour facilities etc. Can the FACCHC control the destruction of railway property? It is unlikely that it currently has the legal authority; and even if it did, it is debatable whether it would have the time to grapple with such a monumental subject.

That is not altogether surprising, not only because of the FACCHC's short history, but also because some observers believe that the threat to railway and harbour property can be handled by provincial instead of federal authorities. Until recently, such land had been assumed to be beyond the reach of provincial statutes, including heritage statutes; however, recent jurisprudence to the contrary suggests that provincial conservation officials could try to protect this property; the result, however, could be a rip-roaring constitutional battle.

Some conservationists would like to avoid such a mess by persuading the federal agencies (such as The Canadian Transport Commission) who supervise these lands to control the destruction of heritage in the course of their other activities. However, the mandate of the various agencies established to regulate the use of such properties sometimes appears too narrow, under current legislation, to include heritage conservation. Consequently, there is currently little control upon the destruction of heritage on those properties; but fortunately, more and more noises are being heard in the corridors of these federal agencies to the effect that their mandate will eventually be "re-interpreted" to justify a more considerate approach.

Some people are not waiting. One M.P. has submitted a Private Member's Bill to the House of Commons; this Bill would give Canada a statute similar to the American system. As mentioned earlier, the U.S. environmental impact system applies to federally-subsidized works as well as to the projects of the government itself; consequently, railways would be subject to such controls, and no railway station could be demolished without special reports being filed and citizens given a chance to object.

The main thrust of this Bill, however, would be felt upon projects of the federal government itself; most pundits give it the same chances of success as the Toronto Blue Jays in the World Series. Nevertheless, some Canadian conservationists firmly believe that sooner or later, Canada will follow suit and place enforceable *legal* controls on its own destruction of heritage and that of the works it supervises. Whether that prediction comes true or whether Canada continues to rely on purely administrative techniques is yet to be seen, but the future promises to be most interesting for Canada's federal heritage legislation.

THE WORLD HERITAGE CONVENTION

It was mentioned earlier that as of July 1976, federal documents were still saying that the federal government had no heritage policy. That same month, Canada took another step to remedy that situation.

On July 23rd, 1976, Canada officially adhered to the *World Heritage Convention,* drafted in Paris in 1972. The Convention states that the signatories are formally committed to the protection of heritage within and even beyond their borders.

This was not the first international treaty of this kind. In 1954, the *Convention for the Protection of Cultural Property in the Event of Armed Conflict* was drafted in The Hague and was accepted by most eastern and western block countries. Each signatory promised to respect the designated heritage sites of other countries. Canada never signed this Convention, but accepted a similar obligation when it adhered to the *World Heritage Convention.*

These obligations to respect the sites of other countries create some unusual legal oddities. As mentioned earlier, Canada's commitment to *its own* heritage is administrative, not statutory. Technically speaking, the Canadian federal government is in the curious position of being *less legally committed* to the protection of Canadian landmarks than is the government of Outer Mongolia, San Marino, Norway, the U.S.S.R. or any other signatory of the Conventions.

This was already the case before 1976 under the Hague Convention of 1954; but the situation became even stranger in 1976 when Canada joined the countries adhering to the *World Heritage Convention.* The federal government became legally bound to respect heritage sites on *foreign* soil, even though the federal government recognizes no legal obligation to respect heritage sites on *Canadian* soil: Canadian heritage sites are not owed the same attention as Canada legally owes to, say, the Statue of Liberty or Big Ben.

Canada not only owes a greater legal duty to foreign monuments than to its own, but foreign governments are also under a greater legal duty to Canadian monuments than is the Canadian government

Some observers argue that these are technicalities which are of interest only to twisted legal minds; others argue that they are flies in the proverbial ointment which the federal government must take care of, if only for the sake of consistency. The latter argument has also been used to support environmental assessment legislation along American lines, i.e. a *statute* which would *oblige* the federal government to respect Canadian heritage in the same way that the Convention obliges us to respect foreign heritage. It remains to be seen whether the federal government will act upon these recommendations, or whether these curiosities will remain on the books to relieve the boredom of future generations of law students.

THE PROVINCIAL GOVERNMENTS

(i) Legal Basis

Eight of Canada's ten provincial governments have empowered their officials to grant permanent protection to heritage sites, both public and private. The only two exceptions are Ontario and Nova Scotia.

HERITAGE LEGISLATION AT THE PROVINCIAL LEVEL

	Recommended by Unesco	Newfoundland	Prince Edward Island
Are clear criteria given for the definition of Heritage Property?	Not discussed	No	No
Must notice be given of impending demoliton of unregistered Heritage Property?	Not discussed	No	No
Is Government under any obligation to attempt to protect unregistered Heritage Property?	Yes	Unclear	No
Can demolition of unclassified building be delayed pending study?	Yes	Yes	No
Can definitive protection against demolition be given to a building (short or expropriation)?	Yes	Yes	Yes
Is radius around monument protected?	Yes	No	No
Can governmental decisions on designation be appealed to higher authority by statute?	Yes	No	No
Is the definitive preservation of districts specifically foreseen?	Yes	Unclear	Law Protects "Areas"
Can maintenance of Heritage Property be enforced by the Province?	Yes	No	Yes
Can Heritage Sites be Inspected?	Yes	Archaeological Sites only	Archaeological Sites Only
Does government have right of first refusal on sale of Heritage Buildings?	Not Discussed	No	No
Can Heritage Properties be exempted from building codes?	Yes	No	No
Can illegally altered Heritage Building be restored at owner's expense?	Yes	No	No
What is the maximum penalty for offences?	Not specified	$1000 plus 3 months	$1000

* The law empowers protection of "sites", which can be as large as a district.

(July 1, 1978)

Nova Scotia	New Brunswick	Quebec	Ontario	Manitoba	Saskatchewan	Alberta	British Columbia
No	No	No	No	No	No	No	No
No	No	No	No	No	Yes	No	Indian archaeological site only
No	No	No	Sometimes	No	Unclear	Archaeological Sites only	No
No	No	Yes	Yes	No	Yes	Yes	Yes
No	Yes	Yes	Archaeological Sites Only	Yes	Yes	Yes	Yes
No	No	Yes	No	No	No	No	No
No	No	No	No	No	No	No	No
No	*	Yes	No	*	*	*	*
No	No	Yes	No	No	Unclear	Yes	No
No	No	Yes	Yes	During Work Only	Unclear	Yes	Yes
No	No	Yes	No	No	"Objects" Only	Yes	No
No	No	No	No	No	No	Yes	No
Not applicable	No	Yes	Yes	Subsidized buildings only	Yes	Yes	Yes
Not applicable	$100 plus 30 days	$25,000	$10,000 plus 1 year	$100	$5000 plus 6 months plus damages	$50,000 plus 1 year plus damages	$2,000 plus 6 months

STATUTES FOR PROVINCIAL HERITAGE PROTECTION

ALBERTA: The Alberta Historical Resources Act
BRITISH COLUMBIA: The Heritage Conservation Act
MANITOBA: The Historic Sites and Objects Act
NEW BRUNSWICK: The Historic Sites Protection Act
NEWFOUNDLAND: The Historic Objects, Sites and Records Act
PRINCE EDWARD ISLAND: The Recreation Development Act and the Archaeological Investigation Act
QUEBEC: The Cultural Property Act
SASKATCHEWAN: The Saskatchewan Heritage Act and The Provincial Parks, Protected Areas, Recreation Sites and Antiquities Act

This legislative smorgasbord is outlined in the accompanying chart.

Nova Scotia's *Historical Objects Protection Act* controls only archaeological excavations on government land. The more recent Nova Scotia *Historic Properties Designation Act* does not control alteration or demolition on properties so "designated". Ontario's unusual situation is described in Chapter 6.

(ii) Some Features of Canadian Legislation

In most of Canada, provincial governments are vested with the primary responsibility for protecting heritage. They usually have special statutes specifically for that purpose. The accompanying chart summarizes the contents of those statutes. The main feature of most of these statutes is that they authorize provincial governments to designate heritage sites, and then to prohibit any alterations or demolition on those sites unless ministerially approved.

(iii) Surroundings

What happens when someone decides to stuff construction all around a heritage site? The only province to protect the surroundings of designated sites is Quebec: the distance is a radius of 500 feet. Any projects within 1/2 mile of a designated site in Alberta must, according to regulations passed under the Alberta *Planning Act,* be submitted for comment to officials of that province; but their decision is not legally binding.

The effect of a heritage structure can be lost in an unsympathetic environment such as that of Halifax's Old Dutch Church

(iv) Groups and Districts

For some time, most authorities have agreed that the potential for heritage conservation is best found in the protection of entire districts: that is where the most benefits can result. Nevertheless, only one provincial statute refers specifically to the provincial protection of districts: the Quebec *Cultural Property Act* empowers the Minister to declare protected districts.

The New Brunswick Minister of Education can also designate "historic districts". There is only one small problem: the designation has no legal effect.

The other provincial statutes do not refer specifically to districts; instead, they usually refer to *"sites"*. A "site" can be as large or as small as the government declares it to be. An entire district can be considered a single site for legal purposes. The Alberta government has recently decided to protect a "site" which includes some sixty buildings, and two British Columbia "sites" (Gastown and Chinatown in Vancouver) each contain even more properties and a multitude of owners.

(v) Procedure

The tedious procedure for designation usually comprises a number of steps, not all of which are described in legislation; some are hidden in Cabinet Regulations, and others are simply carried out in practice without any formal legal requirement. They apply more or less to all provinces except Nova Scotia and Ontario (described later).

Most provinces have historical boards which advise the government regarding structures worthy of protection; but only in Quebec and Alberta is it obligatory for the government to consult with the board.

The owner of a property proposed for protection is usually *notified* beforehand of this possibility; this is a legal requirement in both Alberta and Quebec, where such notice must be given sixty days before designation. This notice must include the reasons for the proposed designation.

Once the property has been designated for protection, it is usually customary to register this fact at the friendly neighborhood land titles office. This is a legal requirement in Alberta, P.E.I. and Quebec. P.E.I. adds that the designation must be announced in a local newspaper and be posted on a sign on the property.

No provincial statute outlines an elaborate procedure for applications to conduct alterations or demolition on designated heritage sites. There are precious few designated buildings in Canada, and even fewer applications to change them; consequently, this activity is usually treated in an *ad hoc* manner.

HERITAGE & PROVINCIAL POLICY

In most provinces, heritage enjoys no more protection from provincial public works than it does from federal works. Again, the toll on heritage has been considerable. As usual, however, many provinces have set up interdepartmental committees to supervise public works which affect heritage property.

Two provinces which will "force" themselves to consider cultural property in their planning process are Ontario and Alberta. The Ontario *Environmental Assessment Act 1975* and two Alberta statutes (the *Historical Resources Act* and the *Land Surface Conservation & Reclamation Act*) have been enacted, along with an assortment of Cabinet Regulations to implement them. Those laws and regulations state that various public authorities *must*, prior to relevant public works projects, submit a detailed assessment of their impact upon the environment including cultural property. Public hearings are also foreseen.

An interesting feature of this legislation is that the requirement for environmental impact assessments can extend to large private projects as well as governments. In Alberta, for example, all oil drilling must be accompanied by archaeological inspection.

Archaeology has, however, sometimes become such a preoccupation in the environmental impact assessments that some authorities have forgotten that other kinds of

The arterial road which was ripping through the heart of St. John's (above) was finally stopped by citizen protest. However, protest did not save the historic Brackman Ker Mill in Edmonton's Strathcona disrict: while the order to protect it waited for one Minister's signature, another Minister ordered bulldozers in on a Saturday evening and reduced it to rubble (below).

heritage sites (e.g. buildings) are also entitled to some attention. In Ontario, this disregard for existing heritage buildings in the environmental assessment process has even been written into the Cabinet Regulations.

These Regulations represent, in general, a significant contribution to Canadian environmental law; but like all new legislation there are some bugs in them. Those bugs are found in the treatment of demolition. The Regulations now stipulate that a project is exempt from environmental assessment if it deals only with the "retirement" of a building. According to the Senior Environmental Planner of the Environmental Approvals Branch of the Environmental Assessment and Planning Division of the Ontario Ministry of the Environment, who is presumably an authority on "environment", demolitions are thereby excluded from the environmental assessment process: it appears that Ontario does not demolish buildings, it "retires" them. The fact that it presents these buildings with a wrecking ball or a stick of dynamite instead of a gold watch is irrelevant. One wonders whether the officials who drafted these regulations would enjoy being "retired" in the same fashion.

Consequently, the integration of heritage conservation into provincial policy does not have any more legal teeth to it than heritage conservation at the federal level. Like the latter, it must rely upon internal administrative procedures. The strength of these procedures varies from province to province; yet at no time in the past has there been such optimism concerning the future of conservation in provincial policy.

The Canadian Council of Resource and Environment Ministers is a prestigeous organization which was founded recently to permit top federal and provincial environmental officials to compare notes. The Council has now undertaken a serious study of environmental impact legislation and procedures, and many observers believe that a major strengthening of environmental policies will be the direct result. If these predictions are correct, then it is likely that heritage conservation will share in the benefits.

CHAPTER 5

SELECTED PROBLEMS IN PROVIN-CIAL LEGISLATION

GENERAL

The chart displayed in the previous Chapter indicates some of the major features of provincial legislation in Canada. Conservationists familiar with the legislation in many other jurisdictions might be tempted to agree with the conservationist who asserted that "our legislation is so full of holes that it could have been engraved on Swiss cheese". That view is perhaps extreme; but some areas are coming under increasing scrutiny.

EXAMPLES OF AREAS OF CONCERN

(i) Maintenance

Most provinces do not enforce maintenance of designated heritage sites. In Kingston, a former home of Sir John A. Macdonald's family was left to fall into such disrepair that the commemorative plaque was removed in disgust.

(ii) Building Codes

Many conservationists who have bright-eyed and bushy-tailed ideas for the renovation of heritage buildings get a rude jolt when they encounter their friendly local building inspector. Renovations must frequently attain such high standards (e.g. National Building Code standards) that even the most dedicated heritage nut takes his football and goes home.

Most provinces do not compel the maintenance of heritage buildings such as this Victoria landmark

Strict compliance with building codes is a constant problem: only Alberta empowers its Minister to waive building code provisions, but this is done only in exceptional circumstances.

The National Building Code, which is the model for building codes throughout the country, specifically permits building inspectors to grant "equivalents", i.e. to approve buildings which do not meet the wording of the Code but are otherwise *as safe* as the Code buildings. Inspectors, however, are loath to make such decisions: for if there is a fire, the public will tend to blame *them* instead of the Code.

The practical impact of this problem varies from one municipality to another. In some municipalities, building inspectors automatically refuse any project which does not comply textually with the National Building Code; in others, trade-offs are possible. The degree to which inspectors will exercise such discretion will vary with the personality of each inspector, and the side of the bed he woke up on.

Conservationists hope to overcome the building code problem without sacrificing safety: they do not want to fry anyone, particularly themselves. The most direct way of achieving this purpose would be for the federal and provincial governments (both of which are involved in drafting codes) to elaborate upon the scope of "equivalents" which are possible in heritage structures and thus give more guidance for building inspectors. Furthermore, these governments can increase their advisory service for specific proposed equivalents where building inspectors are stumped or reluctant to make a decision. This advisory service already exists in a federal agency: it is still small and relatively unknown, but is a useful body to which building inspectors can occasionally pass the proverbial buck. It is called:

The Fire Research Section
National Research Council
Montreal Road
Ottawa, Ontario

(iii) Enforcement

Despite the fact that governments were specifically empowered to control demolition on private property, action has been slow in coming. Only two provinces, Quebec and Alberta, have geared their administrative machinery to place several dozen buildings on the protected list every year.

Until recently, Alberta declared that it would not protect a single building without acquiring it. Manitoba's statute was in existence for ten years before officials decided to protect the first privately owned property in November 1975. In Saskatchewan, the only Canadian province to demand that notice be given of impending demolition of interesting sites, there is no record within the past ten years of such notice ever being given or even requested.

A statute is worthless unless it is implemented. In Canada, four legal obstacles stand in the way of citizens

trying to persuade governments to enforce their own
laws:

   a) No heritage statute gives citizens any right to
      compel government to protect a component of our
      heritage;

   b) Citizens have no right to governmental informa-
      tion concerning implementation of laws;

   c) Citizens have no right to deduct expenses from
      taxable income when those expenses are incurred
      to protect the "public interest"; by contrast, all
      expenses to promote the private interest and profit
      (including lobbying) are tax-deductible;

   d) Citizens have no inherent right to legal action
      even when the public interest is being harmed by
      blatantly illegal acts.

These four problems are the primary obstacles to
effective public participation in the conservation of
Canada's heritage.

The first problem is self-explanatory; the others
deserve more explanation. They are called respectively
the access to information problem, the lobbying problem,
and the *locus standi* problem. They are discussed further
below.

(iv) Access to Information

In some countries, such as the United States, all
governmental information is presumed *public until declared confidential;* if it is declared confidential, there
must be a valid reason. Otherwise, the courts may force
the government to release the information under the
Freedom of Information Act.

Such government information has been essential for
citizens' groups to gather information for a wide assortment of public campaigns. The heritage movement has
been no exception: access to governmental information
has been essential in saving many structures, particularly those threatened by public works.

Canada presents a different picture. If Ralph Nader
had been working in Canada, he would still be driving a
Corvair.

Under the Canadian *Official Secrets Act*, all governmental information in Canada is *secret until approved for distribution*. Such approval is at the sole *discretion* of the government. There is no way that citizens can compel the issue of government information related to heritage conservation or any other subject.

This book is not the place to become involved in a harangue over the complicated issue of freedom of information: first, the problem has been discussed at length elsewhere; second, it appears to be decreasing in the heritage field. Projects such as National Harbours Board plans for old dock facilities are no longer shrouded in the secrecy that used to characterize them; furthermore, the federal government's Throne Speech as far back as 1976 promised that definite action would be taken to make such information more available. Consequently, conservationists hope that the days when they could be caught off guard by harmful plans and projects will soon be over.

(v) Lobbying

Despite the fact that the conservation movement is acquiring more eloquent gremlins every day, there is a great deal of difficulty in counterbalancing the lobbying ability of speculators and developers. Many of the misconceptions concerning conservation are being actively promoted by these "vested interests". Occasionally, speculators and developers have even succeeded in persuading legislators that public opinion opposes heritage conservation, as when a southern Ontario politician predicted that conservation of a local landmark would cause rioting in the streets.

It is difficult to quantify the amount of lobbying which speculators and developers have engaged in throughout our multitudinous levels of government. In one province, newspapers were filled with rumors of prominent former politicians being dispatched to the provincial capital with enormous sums of money in briefcases to forestall the preservation of two invaluable landmarks.

It should be remembered at this juncture that under section 20(1) (cc) of the *Income Tax Act*, all the developers' and speculators' *lobbying expenses are tax-deductible;* indeed, one prominent Montreal tax expert maintains quite seriously that bribes are tax-deductible . . . provided that one can produce receipts.

There is only one criterion for deductibility: the taxpayer must show that he is lobbying for a mercenary purpose. By contrast, lobbying on behalf of the *public interest* is *not tax-deductible;* and if a public interest group is accused of lobbying, *it is liable to lose its registration as a tax-deductible charity.* Under such circumstances, it is no surprise that conservationists have had a hard time making their voice heard in provincial capitals, and persuading officials to give full effect to the heritage legislation at their disposal.

There is no indication of any governmental study being given to this problem.

(vi) Locus Standi

Conservationists used to believe our textbooks which proclaim that age-old rights such as those listed in Magna Carta are sacred: Article 40 of the Magna Carta says "To no man shall . . . I deny justice": the king and his courts would not deprive citizens of their right to protection under the "Rule of Law".

Times have changed.

Apparently, Article 40 of the Magna Carta can now be treated as a dead letter in Canadian courts. Although it gives the impression that citizens have a *right* to protection under the law, Canadian courts often demand that litigants *prove* they have a right to such protection, failing which the protection is denied.

This tack is taken in the name of *"Locus Standi"*, a latin phrase which attempts to lend respectability to one of the strangest doctrine ever invoked by Canadian courts: if an individual is harmed illegally, he can sue; but if all the other members of the community are also harmed equally, they all lose their right to sue.

93

King John and the Barons who wrote Magna Carta; inset, Sir Charles Fitzpatrick who helped rewrite it.

This judicial invention emerged in the latter part of the nineteenth century, when some judges started to complain about their workload. They said that if they had to listen to cases where all kinds of members of a community were being harmed, there would be a "flood of litigation" and they would become overworked. Since this would be "against the public interest", they simply refused to listen to any cases wherein entire communities were being harmed. If "the public interest" was at stake, they said, then the government (or Attorney General's office) should look after it; the courts would not, whether illegalities were involved or not.

The notion that citizens had to look to government for protection instead of looking to the law was new, and not very helpful on occasions when it was government itself which was being accused of the illegality.

Nevertheless, *"locus standi"* became accepted. When it was challenged in the 1915 case of *Robertson v. City of Montreal*, Chief Justice Fitzpatrick of the Supreme Court of Canada added another reason for disregarding "public interest" cases: "The city would never be free from litigation with its attendant expense when, as would probably be often the case, the complainants were men of straw".

After exactly seven hundred years of repeating that "the law is no respector of persons", the judiciary thereby permitted a unique policy of *prejudging* litigants and of *disregarding* their arguments accordingly.

The notion that critics of government were vaguely contemptible was not peculiar to the Chief Justice. It was also implicit in other systems of government against which Canada fought two world wars. That did not, however, change jurisprudence: it was the Chief Justice's statement which was cited with approval in one Canadian court after another, up to the present day. The doctrine has cost the conservation movement court battles, such as the fight to save Van Horne's house in Montreal.

Conservationists have challenged this doctrine, but

the Supreme Court of Canada again ruled in 1976 that alleged illegalities such as tampering with Ontario's protected Elora Gorge by a conservation authority were none of the citizens' business. Some conservationists have given up on the judicial system and hope to redress grievances through the provincial legislature. Others, such as Prince Edward Islander Mario Carota, have challenged the *locus standi* problem in new litigation (this time arising in Summerside), and continue to fight the issue in court again and again. Carota, who is not a lawyer but who argues his cases himself, has taken his lawbooks wrapped in cardboard and string to almost every level of judiciary . . . and has occasionally defeated government lawyers who appeared with literally truckloads of texts.

Conservationists know that their legal rights are illusory unless they can be invoked in the crunch of a legal battle. Consequently, citizens' groups are keeping their eyes on the Elora Gorge lobbyists and the continuing saga of Mario Carota's litigeous crusade in the hope that their right to protection under the rule of law will be reinstated.

Montreal's Van Horne Mansion, a victim of Locus Standi: the legality of its demolition, said the judge, was none of the conservationists' business.

THE DEEPER ROOTS OF SUCH PROBLEMS

(i) General

With the exception of Monaco, Canada has been virtually the last western country to take part in the conservation of cultural property. There are still parts of Canada where effective legislation is non-existent. Even where legislation does exist, implementation remains a problem.

There are some cynics who argue that as long as governments are the largest developers and wreckers in Canada, heritage legislation is a lost cause from the outset. Conservationists may not agree with this conclusion, but they cannot dispute the existence of a certain conflict of interest. Nevertheless, it would be misleading and totally defeatist to assume that questions relating to heritage conservation in Canada can be reduced to the issue of governmental self-interest. The broader issues are discussed below.

A recurring problem is faced by conservationists whenever they request governments to protect any structure. There is so much soul-searching and research which is imposed upon limited governmental staffs that only a tiny minority of worthy buildings can be studied and placed upon the inventory of protected structures.

How does one explain Canada's profound reticence regarding the protection of landmarks and neighbourhoods? The customary answer is inexperience; and this is in part true. Canada, unlike most other countries, does not have a background of legislative precedents on which to build new legislation for the conservation of its historic and architectural heritage. Saskatchewan provides a good example: government officials in that province had many foresighted ideas concerning the direction of legislative reform, but the awkward legal draftsmanship of the *Saskatchewan Heritage Act* has created severe problems of implementation which have taken months to unravel.

If this were the only obstacle to effective heritage legislation, then Canada's problems could soon be solved:

there is a consistently growing stream of information relating to conservation which is reaching our government officials, and for which Heritage Canada and other conservation organizations can legitimately claim some credit.

Inexperience, however, does not entirely explain the situation. Emerging countries with far less legislative experience than Canada's have enacted more sophisticated statutes by looking beyond their boundaries to international precedent. The government of one West Indian country, for example, invited UNESCO advisors to help draft its new heritage legislation. By contrast, legislatures in Canada have frequently exercised a kind of willful blindness to international precedents, ostensibly based upon the sublimely parochial notion that their problems bore no resemblance to those of anywhere else in the world.

This blindness to precedent even extends to the experience of other provinces within Canada. For example, in 1963 the Province of Quebec abandoned the legal program entitled "voluntary designation". Under that program, the only private landmarks protected were those which the owner agreed with the government to protect. After some forty years of mediocre results, the program was abandoned in favour of more sophisticated legislation, which in turn was improved again in 1972. In 1975, however, two provinces simultaneously claimed to have "discovered" the voluntary designation scheme, and proposed it as the ultimate answer to their conservation problems.

This reticence is now being challenged not only by conservationists, but even by officials within governments themselves. It is likely that Canadian governments will take a more positive approach to the implementation of heritage legislation; but to do so, they must grapple with difficulties which run much deeper than "inexperience". Those difficulties are of a social, economic and ideological nature.

(ii) The Social Problem

On the social level, the problem is basically a question of public education; there are many people, even in high office, who see no purpose in preserving history. They use the expression "beauty is in the eye of the beholder" to condemn as subjective and arbitrary any favourable assessment of a masterpiece. In their hands, no achievement of civilization is safe.

Even more dangerous are those who applaud the deliberate destruction of history. They fall into two

Ontario officials gleefully begin demolition at the Don Jail

categories. First, there are those who, as true children of a consumer society, unthinkingly approve every replacement of the old by the new, or the small by the big, regardless of quality. To them, the replacement of something small and beautiful by something big and new is by definition progress. There is a second and more vicious category who read bizarre ideological implications into the destruction of heritage. Such are those who applaud the demolition of fine homes because these structures symbolize the "robber barons" or "idle rich"; one is also reminded of the public official who hailed the destruction of one of Montreal's finest churches by the

Université du Québec as symbolizing "the triumph of education over clericalism". When discussing conservation with officials such as these, one must feel a certain sympathy for the position of Pope Leo I when he tried reasoning with Attila the Hun.*

This is a problem which can only be solved by intensified efforts in the field of public education, reinforced by effective legislation. The conservation movement is working in this direction, and the growing number of sympathetic officials is evidence of success.

(iii) The Economic Problem

Until recently, there was an unshakeable belief among public officials, particularly at the municipal level, that the destruction and redevelopment of sites was beneficial for the municipal economy.

This misconception is somewhat easier to deal with than the social problem mentioned above, since remedial information can be addressed to a smaller audience, namely the Canadian economic and governmental communities. This is a task which has been eagerly taken on by Canadian conservationists, as evidenced by increased presentations to relevent conventions and general meetings. Part of the "sales pitch" is mentioned in Chapter 2.

(iv) The Ideological Problem

A further obstacle to effective legislation has been a form of ideological mythology surrounding the free enterprise system.

Conservation of landmarks and neighbourhoods implies a restriction upon property rights, and is thereby equated with the "collapse of free enterprise" etc. This is postulated as a self-evident principle of our capitalist system.

---

* Historical footnote: If it is any consolation, one may note that Leo succeeded. Conservationists trust that Canadian decision-makers will act at least as civilized as Attila did.

The basic concern of proprietors, of course, isn't abstract philosophy: it's money. Owners are worried about heritage legislation because heritage controls might affect the marketability of their property. This is a serious issue which many conservationists would prefer to forget; proprietors have no intention of letting them do so, and hence a chorus of denunciations can be heard based upon "free enterprise", the law etc. It might come as something of a surprise to conservationists to learn that the owners do not have any technically reliable authority on which to base their complaint; that does not, however, solve the problem. Sooner or later, conservationists must come to grips with the issue of the financial position of owners of designated property; but that decision should be based upon the proper reasons (described later) not upon the misconceptions described below.

The first issue is the allegation that heritage conservation is incompatible with the philosophical principles of our capitalist system as handed down to us by the great thinkers of the early nineteenth century.

Edmund Burke would be appalled to behold the arguments being made in his name and in the defence of private property. The political philosophy developed by Locke, Burke, Jefferson and others had the explicit purposes of *defending residents* against governmental expulsion and to protect the common heritage of communities. Burke even defended the infamous "Rotten borough" system because he clung to the traditional character of communities. The writings of eighteenth century philosophers are now being quoted out of context to justify the *dislocation* of individuals and entire neighbourhoods by unwanted redevelopment. This is the diametric opposite of the purpose which those writers espoused.

This text is not the place to undertake an elaborate rebuttal of the equation between heritage conservation and the red menace. The equation rests upon the notion that controls upon the use of property are unprecedented

101

and unjustified in a free enterprise system . . . a notion whose falsehood has been demonstrated many times before. Suffice it to say that there is nothing in the philosophy of private property which suggests that property can be used for *any* purpose whatsoever. To use the phrase of the Quebec Civil Code, property rights have *always* been subject to "public order and good morals". If one is performing an act which is contrary to the interests of the community, the fact that one is doing it on private property has *always* been and still is ~~totally~~ irrelevant. *Secondary*

The equation between land use controls and the demise of free enterprise becomes increasingly incredible when one notes the jurisdictions in which conservation legislation is enforced. The city of Washington has had stringent land use controls since the 1790's; does that make it the oldest hotbed of socialism in North America? Furthermore, the United States conserves more land-marks and neighbourhoods than its legislation would suggest: many state laws do *not specifically authorize* officials to conserve historic districts, but almost every state has taken the initiative of doing so anyway by an ingenious and aggressive extension to the rules of municipal law. By contrast, Canadian officials have often failed to use protective legislation even when Canadian laws *specifically empowered* them to do so. We're not "subversives" here, not like those Americans.

Another argument frequently heard in Canada is that the designation of heritage buildings is tantamount to an unacceptable public expropriation without compensation. This argument presupposes that a landowner is, in law, vested with a basic unfettered right to dispose of his land as he chooses, and that any restriction on that right is exceptional and at least partly confiscatory. This is not the place to launch a wild and woolly debate over the desirability of such a proposition; however, it should be pointed out that the foregoing assumption is not technically correct, nor has it ever been technically correct. The law has *never* treated land as a commodity which could be traded at will like other goods: landowners have never been able to invoke unfettered rights of ownership, at least since the time of William the Conqueror. For example, as little as 150 years ago, foreigners were not even permitted to inherit land or leave it in their will in many parts of Canada. Zoning has been recognized as a valid restriction on land since the turn of the century, and it is settled law that downzoning (i.e. more restrictive zoning) does not entitle the owner to any compensation. Consequently, the notion that the land use controls such as heritage designations are exceptional and confiscatory has no legal leg to stand on.

One also hears the claim that the state has no business affecting the market value of an owner's property. As mentioned above, that claim is rejected by Canadian law every time that land is downzoned; indeed, the Canadian government dramatically affects the price of *everything* whenever it adopts policies such as those relating to the Canadian dollar.

Consequently, if a heritage designation affects the marketability of a property, the proprietor has no ground for complaint in the strictly legalistic sense. That doesn't make him feel any happier, however; and a conservationist who relies exclusively on this technical analysis will probably earn few brownie points in the political forum. Disregard for the frustration of landowners may be acceptable in Europe where such frustration earns remarkably little sympathy; but in Canada, some "appeasement" is politically necessary sooner or later.

Chapter 11 describes some of the financial and schemes which have been instituted for heritage sites. Developers and speculators consider them a drop in the proverbial bucket.

Chapter 10 describes the current and potential tax position of heritage buildings. Many conservationists earnestly hope that tax incentives will eventually make it economically interesting for even speculators to invest in designated heritage buildings. However, even if such incentives materialize, they are at best far down the road. In the meantime, owners continue to grumble about heritage legislation.

This is where political risks become unavoidable. If conservationists and authorities choose to wait until fancy economic schemes become available for designated heritage, they may be left with little heritage to protect. Unless they are prepared to sacrifice a significant component of our heritage to the daily ravages now taking place, they have no choice but to fight a "holding action" by immediately designating sites at the risk of upsetting the owner, in the hope that the owner can be appeased at some point in the future.

The province with the most experience in designations is Quebec, and the political risks of widespread designation have turned out to be smaller than those probably anticipated. When all these "ideological" factors are weighed, conservationists appear justified in continuing to press for the implementation of heritage statutes.

CHAPTER 6

LOCAL AUTHORITIES

MUNICIPAL POWERS

(i) General

Municipal legislation in Canada is not really a three-ringed circus; it just looks that way. In reality, one can neatly lump together three kinds of legislation which confer powers on Canadian municipalities for heritage purposes.

The first kind is "enabling legislation" which gives special powers to *all* municipalities in a given province for the protection of heritage. The second confers powers on only certain *specified* municipalities. The third is ordinary planning legislation which can (with imagination) be adapted for the protection of heritage property.

The accompanying chart summarizes municipal legislation which is of direct relevance to heritage conservation. It can be argued that the extent of municipal powers in this field is a pleasant surprise: few Canadian conservationists are aware that municipalities from coast to coast have been vested with such powers.

This lack of awareness of municipal powers, however, is itself predictable: *virtually all powers enacted specifically for heritage purposes have been bestowed within the last five years.*

If some observers are still wondering whether Canada is enjoying some momentum in heritage legislation, the foregoing point should settle the issue.

Again, it must nevertheless be pointed out that all new legislation has its ups and downs. When a large

HERITAGE LEGISLATION FOR MUNICIPALITIES

(July 1, '78)

| | NEWFOUNDLAND | | PRINCE EDWARD ISLAND | | |
---	St John's	Elsewhere	Charlottetown	Elsewhere	Sherbrooke Village
Is heritage conservation an obligatory part of municipal planning?	No	No	No	No	Yes
Is municipality obliged to file environmental impact assessment on demolition of heritage?	No	No	No	No	No
Can municipality give permanent protection to buildings	Yes	Unclear	Yes	No	Yes
Can municipality give temporary protection to buildings	Yes	Unlikely	Yes	No	Yes
Can municipality regulate					
Bulk and Height	Yes	Unclear	Yes	Yes	Yes
Design	Yes	Unclear	Yes	Yes	Yes
Use	Yes	Yes	Yes	Yes	Yes
Set-back	Yes	Yes	Yes	Yes	Yes
Signs	Yes	Yes	Unclear	Yes	Yes
Can municipality accept or reject applications for construction on heritage sites on a discretionary basis	Yes	No	Probably	No	Yes
Can municipality enforce maintenance					
a) of dwelling interiors	Yes	Yes	Yes	Yes	Yes
b) of dwelling exteriors	Yes	Unclear	Yes	Yes	Yes
c) of non-residential interiors	No	Unclear	Unclear	Yes	Yes
d) of non-residential exteriors	No	Unclear	Yes	Yes	Yes
Can municipality compel					
a) protection of trees	Yes	Yes	Unclear	Unclear	Uncle
b) landscaping	No	No	No	No	No
Can illegally altered building be restored at owner's expense?	Yes	Yes	No	No	Uncle
Usual maximum penalty for offences	$100	$100-$200	$90 + 90 days	$500 + 90 days	$500

[1] Except in Peggy's Cove
[2] Except in municipalities regulated by the Cities & Towns Act
[3] Except under development control schemes
[4] Except in Montreal, Quebec, and rural municipalities

NOVA SCOTIA	NEW BRUNSWICK	QUEBEC	ONTARIO	MANITOBA		SASKATCHEWAN	ALBERTA	BRITISH COLUMBIA
Elsewhere				Winnipeg	Elsewhere			
No[1]	Yes	No	No	Yes	Yes	No	No	No
No	No	No	Not Yet	No	No	No	Not Yet	No
No	Yes	No	No	Yes	No	No	Yes	Yes
No	Yes	Yes	Yes	Yes	No	No	Yes	Yes
Yes	Yes	Yes	Yes	Yes	Yes	Yes	Yes	Yes
Yes	Yes	Yes	Yes	Yes	Yes	No	Yes	Yes
Yes	Yes	Yes	Yes	Yes	Yes	Yes	Yes	Yes
Yes	Yes	Yes	Yes	Yes	Yes	Yes	Yes	Yes
Yes	Yes	Yes	Yes	Yes	Yes	Yes	Yes	Yes
No[1]	Yes	No	Yes	Yes	No	No	Yes	Yes
Yes	Yes	Yes	Yes	Yes	Yes	Yes	Yes	Yes
Yes	Yes	Yes	Yes	Yes	Yes	Yes	Yes	Yes
Yes	No	Yes[2]	Yes	No	No	Unclear	Yes	Yes
Yes	No	Yes[2]	Yes	No	No	Unclear	Yes	Yes
Unclear	Yes	Yes	Yes	Yes	Yes	Yes	Yes	Yes
No	Yes	Yes[4]	No[3]	No	No	No	No	No
No	Yes	No[2]	Yes	Yes	Yes	Yes	No	Unclear
100	$100	Variable	Variable	$1000 + 6 Mths.	$1000 + 6 Mths.	$1000 + 1 Mth.	$500	$2000 + 6 Mths.

province such as Ontario introduces new legislation for municipalities, it is extraordinarily difficult to cover all contingencies in the first effort: some problems simply refuse to be solved on the first try.

In other words, municipal legislation is similar to legislation at all other governmental levels insofar as it covers some issues and misses others. This is no cause for trauma: it is to be expected in a country whose legislative history in the area is so recent. The following are some salient features of this legislation.

(ii) Heritage Legislation on a Province-Wide Basis

Five provinces empower all their municipalities to give some protection to cultural sites.

The British Columbia *Heritage Conservation Act* authorizes municipalities in that province to list properties which will enjoy permanent protection. As mentioned previously, the British Columbia provincial government is also empowered to grant such protection; protection may therefore come from either the province or the municipality. Similar systems have recently been introduced in two other provinces: Alberta has amended its *Alberta Historical Resources Act* accordingly, and New Brunswick has passed the *Municipal Heritage Preservation Act* to supplement its provincial *Historic Sites Protection Act*.

In Ontario, on the other hand, the province protects only archaeological ruins. Any other kind of historic site can be protected only by municipalities. Furthermore, the protection granted by a municipality to a threatened structure can almost never exceed 270 days; after that delay expires, the building can be demolished whether the municipality likes it or not. Consequently, in order to grant indefinite protection to a building, it would be necessary a) to expropriate it, b) to reach an agreement with the proprietor, or c) turn it into an archaeological site by blowing it up.

Quebec empowers municipalities to postpone demolition for a year pending a decision from the Provincial Minister of Cultural Affairs as to whether to give the

108

building permanent protection. Quebec also proposes to grant wider supervisory powers to municipalities in the administration of heritage sites and areas.

(iii) Heritage Legislation of Particular Application

Some provincial governments have given certain *specific* municipalities special powers relating to heritage conservation.

Nova Scotia has granted certain powers in the case of Peggy's Cove, and wider powers to Sherbrooke Village. Newfoundland, Prince Edward Island and Manitoba have granted such powers to their respective capital cities (St. John's, Charlottetown and Winnipeg).

With the exception of Peggy's Cove, all the above municipalities can give *definitive* protection to structures against demolition.

PROTECTION OF DISTRICTS

The new legislation in both Alberta and New Brunswick refers to municipal protection of districts.

In Ontario, the *Ontario Heritage Act* also refers to municipal protection of districts. The municipal plan creating a heritage conservation district must go through a very complicated procedure in which provincial approval must be obtained no less than three times; nevertheless, as in the case of individual structures, protection cannot exceed 270 days for a structure located within such a district. More definitive protection, on the other hand, can be granted under the *Ontario Planning Act*. That statute permits any municipality to refuse a demolition permit indefinitely on *dwellings* in a given zone so long as the applicant refuses to guarantee replacement of the structure by another structure within two years. Although this provision does not protect heritage sites against redevelopment, it can protect them against demolition for parking lots or other such speculative purposes.

Canadian municipalities can take further action by adapting their other land use powers for heritage purposes. That function is described below.

LOCAL LAND USE LEGISLATION

(i) General

Municipalities are empowered to enact land use controls by virtue of enabling legislation passed at the provincial level. Few generalizations can be made aside from the proposition that generalizations are extremely difficult. Procedures and administration of land use controls are subject to various statutes ranging from relative simplicity (one government publication opened with "The first thing that must be said about the municipal system of Prince Edward Island is that there is not a great deal to say about it") to unbelievable complexity. A full analysis would require much more detail, but the following preliminary comments can be made.

(ii) Spatial Aspect of Municipal Controls

Without special legislation, it is very difficult to enact municipal legislation applicable to a single lot: such legislation should generally apply to a wider area. Although the application of by-laws to individual lots (called "spot zoning") has occasionally been upheld by the courts, its legal fate still remains rather unsteady. Consequently, it is preferable to draft any controls in such a way as to apply to a wider area.

(iii) Other Conditions on Validity

Unless special legislation exists, municipal controls usually cannot be discretionary: the by-law itself must clearly outline the maximum obligations of the owner, and no further obligations can be imposed upon him (even by municipal officials) unless they are clearly defined in the by-law. Furthermore, vagueness is a ground on which to challenge the by-law. A partial exception is the new system of "development control", which is starting to be seen in a handful of jurisdictions.

Another important point to remember is that by-laws usually cannot have a retroactive effect. This means that it is impossible to use a new by-law to force an owner to remove a structure or feature of it.

110

Finally, the fact that a municipality has the power to do something does not mean that it can exercise that power under any and all circumstances. Before it can exercise that power, it must usually enact a by-law establishing the administrative procedure for handling that power, its scope, the land area over which it will be exercised etc. Although municipalities cannot legally exceed their powers, they are under no obligation to use the powers they already have.

(iv) Some Important Characteristics

Some powers of municipal governments can be particularly important for heritage purposes.

First, almost all Canadian municipalities are empowered to control bulk and height of buildings. This power is important for two reasons: infill construction in a heritage area should have a bulk and height which does not detract from the character of the area; furthermore, a low permissible building bulk and height will help discourage demolition and redevelopment within the area.

Use is an equally important subject. Almost all Canadian municipalities can control the use of buildings, which is essential in excluding incompatible uses from heritage areas, and in helping stabilize the area's residential component.

Maintenance is another subject which has been included quite recently in the powers of municipalities: most can compel owners to keep a building in decent shape. Some provinces such as British Columbia confer a further power: they permit municipalities to clean up dilapidated buildings at the owner's expense. This power can have a similar effect to maintenance provisions, and in the case of heritage areas might even have greater potential.

The location of a building on a lot can significantly affect the appearance of a streetscape, particularly when it breaks the harmony of a row of buildings. The power to regulate location (or "set-back") is clearly spelled out in all provinces.

Failure to control height can cause visual problems, as this Ottawa street shows; so Ottawa has now downzoned its Centretown area to protect the area's character.

It is obviously desirable to control the design of structures being built or alterations being made in a heritage area. Most provinces specifically empower their municipalities to control design. In such cases, however, the by-law must be sufficiently clear so as to describe exactly what is expected of the owner; in architectural matters, this requirement can cause difficulties in drafting. To meet this problem, some municipalities have requested (and obtained) the exceptional right to establish architectural committees vested with discretion to accept or reject proposals according to their taste. In other jurisdictions, powers are usually more limited e.g. where municipalities must apparently content themselves with controls on façade materials. In some provinces, even the capacity to impose the latter controls is unclear.

The alterations to this Charlottetown house show the importance of design control; so Charlottetown recently vested itself with more sweeping heritage powers.

These pictures illustrate how sign control can effect the appearance of an area

Signs can do a great deal to change the appearance of a heritage area. Every province gives its municipalities the power to regulate signs.

Trees and shrubbery also make a big difference in the appearance of a heritage area. Although few provinces have Quebec's provision which permits municipalities to compel proprietors to plant trees, most municipalities can at least control the destruction of trees, and occasionally shrubs as well.

(v) Implementation

The sanctions imposed upon offenses against municipal by-laws are usually very weak. It is frequently more economical to disregard the by-law and pay the fine than to obey the law. Some municipalities have accordingly turned to the alternative of seeking court injunctions against violators. At first, their capacity to do so was challenged and jurisprudence was divided; but many court decisions now favor the municipality's right to seek injunctions in such cases.

In the case of buildings erected in violation of zoning by-laws, an even more effective resource usually exists,

When the illegal demolition of these heritage homes on Montreal's Drummond Street resulted in a fine of only $10, the city had its Charter changed to provide a more effective deterrent

namely destruction of the building at the owner's expense. Such was recently the case of an enormous (but illegal) highrise project in Hull, Quebec.

If, however, an owner can demonstrate that the application of a by-law to his property is manifestly illogical, most provinces (except Prince Edward Island and Quebec) permit an appeal whereby an exemption (or "variance") can be granted.

115

PROCEDURES

(i) General

All municipal land use controls in Canada are enacted by by-laws. A by-law is enacted by majority vote of a municipal council.

(ii) Notice

Virtually all Canadian jurisdictions insist upon some public notice of changes in land use controls. The delay in which it must be given varies from province to province. This notice gives the citizens an opportunity to attend and speak at the meeting where the proposed changes are discussed, and occasionally where the council actually votes on the proposal.

(iii) Plans

In some provinces land use by-laws are not the only relevant legal mechanism: in addition, plans have legal consequences. In such provinces, a plan is usually not a prerequisite for land use controls of a heritage nature; but if the heritage by-laws contradict the plan, they are open to challenge. In such cases, it is advisable to amend the plan before enacting municipal heritage legislation.

Ontario goes further. Not only are heritage by-laws open to challenge when the plan contradicts them, but they are usually open to challenge even when the plan is silent. An amendment to the plan is an indispensable prerequisite to all area land use controls under the *Ontario Heritage Act,* and to many controls under the *Ontario Planning Act.*

(iv) Other Conditions

The validity of by-laws is subject to a host of conditions mentioned earlier.

In addition, some provinces have established provincial review bodies (called "municipal boards") which can invalidate by-laws on the ground of "unreasonableness". This criterion can include almost anything. The experience of the conservation movement with municipal boards has not been extremely happy: some municipal boards have tended to automatically dismiss all municipal attempts to control urban sprawl or highrise construction as "unreasonable" by definition. Once again, conservationists face a considerable challenge in the field of public information and education; but municipal boards already appear to be warming to heritage.

AUTHORITIES

In those jurisdictions which empower municipalities to protect sites, that protection is exercised by the local municipal council.

HERITAGE AND MUNICIPAL PLANNING POLICY

Only in Manitoba and New Brunswick is it obligatory for municipalities to incorporate heritage conservation in their municipal planning process. This gives conservationists in these provinces some legal basis on which to prod the municipality into some kind of heritage policy.

Even experts disagree, however, as to whether such a plan can legally deter the municipality from botching up a heritage site or district. The replacement of heritage sites by new civic centres has been, to many Canadian mayors, what the pyramid was to Cheops.

In other jurisdictions (e.g. the U.S.), environmental impact legislation has frequently been applied to municipalities to compel them to pay due attention to the heritage resources which they are affecting through public works. It is hoped that Alberta's environmental impact legislation will eventually regulate municipal activity in that way. It is also hoped that Ontario will move in the same direction if it abolishes the assumption that buildings are not demolished, but only "retired".

In the early 1970's, the City of Winnipeg jumped into the forefront of municipal environmental legislation: environmental impact assessments were made obligatory for municipal public works. There was, however, one inconvenience in this heralded law: it had to be obeyed.

117

The City was reminded of this every time it was sued for disregarding the legislation. In court case after court case, it was argued that if the City was in breach of the law, the fault must obviously be with the law and not with the City. To the utter stupefaction of conservationists, several judges accepted this argument: Winnipeg's environmental impact legislation was already a dead letter by the time it was dismantled altogether in 1977.

Winnipeg's City Hall (left) and Ordway's Hall in St. Andrews were both destroyed by municipal authorities. Significantly, these two municipalities have reversed their policy and have become among Canada's foremost proponents of conservation

As usual, conservationists must rely upon the administrative process coming to the rescue. Fortunately, this is certainly the case in Winnipeg (where an excellent heritage plan has been prepared) and in many other Canadian municipalities. Municipal governments from Halifax to Dawson have frequently displayed considerable initiative; whether these efforts will be supplemented by further environmental legislation is a subject which keeps organizations such as the Canadian Council of Resource and Environment Ministers busy, and conservationists are anxious to see the results.

COMMENTARY

(i) The Enforcement Problem Revisited
The fact that several prominent municipalities are tackling heritage problems head-on should not,

nevertheless, lead us to the conclusion that all is rosy in the municipal field. Real problems remain, and are sometimes compounded by judicial interpretations of municipal law. These aspects must be faced squarely.

In order to integrate conservation of heritage property into local planning, there must be some means of enforcement. Among conservationists, one frequently hears the opinion that municipal governments are the most apt to bend the rules concerning proper planning principles. One provincial capital fired every single planner on its staff when the planners joined in criticism of a certain construction project. One study suggested that one third of the sitting members on the municipal councils of major Canadian cities are either developers or agents for developers. Under such circumstances, access to the courts is the only guarantee that proper planning principles will be observed.

That phenomenon returns us to the same dilemma mentioned in the context of provincial legislation: how can citizens have the law enforced if courts refuse to listen to argument? The *locus standi* problem raises its head most frequently in the case of municipal litigation.

Another recurring theme in such municipal litigation is the refusal to listen to citizens' arguments on the basis (of all things) of democracy.

An interesting example of this reasoning is found in a 1975 case whereby the court disregarded citizens' claims that the City of Winnipeg environmental impact regulations (referred to above) were being ignored. In the words of the judge, "this is a case where a few individuals who cannot get the majority of the people to see their point of view are attempting to accomplish the same by making an application to this Court".

It was taken for granted that every decision of municipal politicians represents the will of the majority . . . without any evidence that the public had even been consulted (let alone had approved).

One should note, above all, that the "will of the majority" is irrelevant to one's legal rights and obligations in any system which claims to respect the rule of law. For example, the will of the majority (or even of politicians) has been repeatedly held totally irrelevant when such will was to control real estate development on private (or even public) property. Not only is it ineffectual against vested legal rights, but it is also frequently ineffectual against the "unreasonableness" argument invoked by municipal boards. It sometimes appears that the argument is a one-way street invoked *only* to rebut the claims of conservationists.

If the reaction of Canadian courts to citizens' groups and land use controls continues to be so negative, it is unlikely that the integration of conservation into development policy (at the national, regional or local level) will be enforceable.

Cases such as the Elora Gorge case (mentioned earlier) sank many conservationists into the depths of pessimism, and made some wonder whether the courts would render all legal reform futile. Then came a surprise: the *E.J. Murphy Case* in Victoria. The City of Victoria noticed that a legislative loophole deprived it of needed powers to withhold demolition permits on certain designated heritage buildings. The city concluded that if it could not invoke ordinary powers, it would invoke extra-ordinary ones.

An obscure provision of the B.C. *Municipal Act* said that special powers (including the withholding of permits) could be used in an emergency; so the city declared a *State of Emergency*(!).

When the speculators came out of shock, they attacked the City's action in court in order to obtain their demolition permits. In a remarkable decision, the British Columbia Supreme Court's judgement upheld the City and refused the demolition permits.

Conservationists were elated not only in Victoria, but also throughout Canada, where it is hoped that this case will establish a precedent for heritage litigation in the future. It also renews confidence in the ability of the legal system to protect the heritage of our country.

THE DEEPER ROOTS OF MUNICIPAL RETICENCE

(i) Introduction

The *E.J. Murphy Case* described above resulted from the actions of a municipal council whose audacity was matched only by its ingenuity. But for every heritage oriented council like Victoria's, there are many municipal councils which exhibit the opposite mentality. The same misconceptions and problems which block effective heritage legislation at higher levels are also to be found at the municipal level. There are, however, two major additional problems peculiar to many municipal politicians.

(ii) The Growth Mentality

The first attitude which the conservation movement must overcome is the notion, prevalent among some municipal councils, that *any* growth is a status symbol for the municipality.

Some municipal politicians have equated quantitative growth with personal success and the fulfillment of their mandate, to such an extent that they often use population increase as their main argument for reelection. This attitude is partly attributable to the "bigger-is-better" mentality of a well-trained and gullible consumer society, but is predominantly a holdover from the frontier mentality of past generations: a discriminating attitude toward growth would somehow be treasonable to our manifest destiny. Symptomatic of this mentality was the "curse" which an exasperated politician in a semi-rural suburb of Ottawa levelled at conservationists: "You gotta make up your mind: to live in the country or in the city. As far as I'm concerned, this here is the city. Cities gotta develop. If you don't like it, go live in the woods".

It may take years before such decision-makers can be shown that there is a distinction between quantitative and qualitative growth; some conservationists are tempted to use the pedagogical methods which are allegedly effective with mules; but most are gearing for a long and laborious effort at persuasion.

It would, however, be unfair to those politicians to say that the *only* reason for which they hold this view was because of a mentality which had not progressed beyond the pioneer era. Some hold a more sophisticated view: namely, that growth in general and highrise growth in particular gives the municipalities an aura which could attract investment.

Once upon a time, there was a certain validity to this argument. Canada's "branch-plant economy" is such that most decisions concerning development in general and non-residential development in particular are made at great distances from the location of such development. This leads to intense jockeying among many municipalities to attract the attention of investors, and any growth within the municipality is not only publicized for the sake of publicity, but is also used as proof of an infrastructure capable of accomodating further development. In short, such politicians sought growth because they were convinced that it would become self-generating. This argument was used to justify the demolition of thousands of older structures to make way for the occasional highrise, even in communities which could provide no other economic justification for such a decision.

There was a time when this theory may have been valid for most of Canada, and there may still be areas where (for unusual reasons) it is still valid: but by and large, highrise construction is not the magic honey pot it used to be. There is simply nothing distinctive (and hence worthy of publicity) about highrise growth any more; even shopping centres, which were once considered infallible magnets of development, have become so numerous that the attraction for further investment has been totally diluted. It should be obvious that a "skyline" can no longer possess the distinctive mystical qualities which were once attributed to it.

122

Again, it is up to conservationists to persuade decision-makers of the inescapable new reality: the facile equation between highrise and municipal status has collapsed.

(iii) Municipal Finance

There is an alleged budgetary problem facing heritage conservation. In most of Canada, municipalities raise revenue by levying taxes on the value of land and buildings. The larger and more valuable a building is, the greater will be its tax assessment. This argument has been used to justify the demolition and redevelopment of many heritage sites.

Until recently, there was an unshakable belief among public officials, particularly at the municipal level, that the destruction and redevelopment of sites of architectural or historic interest was beneficial for the municipal economy. This misconception has been firmly refuted by studies conducted by an assortment of experts from Price Waterhouse to Dalhousie University.

Indeed, it would appear that the reverse is true. These same studies have often been able to document cases wherein the marginal cost of servicing new development has exceeded the marginal revenue attributable to redevelopment, resulting in a net loss to the municipality. Furthermore, there are strong indications that Canada's major metropolitan centres (where most such redevelopment takes place) are suffering from inherent "diseconomies of scale" which begin at the level of 500,000 population and intensify thereafter.

By that reasoning, unless Toronto and Montreal adjust their current patterns of development carefully, it is as inevitable for them to eventually face insolvency as it was for New York City.

In that perspective, continued increases in population density through demolition and redevelopment may be against the long term economic interest of those communities. Again, conservationists are continuing to promote this economic research and make the results available to decision-makers. The experience and example of other municipalities which have launched audacious heritage programs (e.g. St. John's Nfld.) can only help in that effort.

PART III
THE POWERS THAT BE

CHAPTER 7

BODIES INVOLVED IN PROTECTION

GENERAL

A list of the bodies in charge of heritage conservation efforts in Canada is drier than a good martini. However, any fearless drudge who proposes to dedicate some time to the conservation problem must familiarize himself with these organizations and agencies, and work with them in the common cause.

GOVERNMENT OFFICIALS

(i) The Federal Level

Two federal departments have overlapping roles in the field of heritage conservation.

The Department of Indian Affairs and Northern Development acquires and promotes national parks, and co-ordinates the federal government's activities relating to heritage sites:

about to be changed

Parks Canada
Department of Indian Affairs & Northern Development
Ottawa, Ontario K1A 0H4

The Secretary of State's Department promotes most aspects of culture other than sites of historic and architectural significance. It also operates the network of

125

national museums, and thereby has a great influence upon archaeological research:

> The Secretary of State
> 66 Slater Street
> Ottawa, Ontario K1A 0M5
> or
> National Museums of Canada
> 300 Laurier Ave. West,
> Ottawa, Ontario K1A 0M8

(ii) The Provincial Level

As mentioned previously, most of the real power in terms of heritage conservation is at the provincial level.

a) Alberta:

> The Minister of Government Services and Culture
> Legislature Building
> Edmonton, Alberta
> or
> Alberta Culture
> 10004 - 104th Street
> Edmonton, Alberta T5J 0K5

b) British Columbia:

> The Minister of Recreation & Conservation
> Parliament Buildings
> Victoria, British Columbia
> or
> Deputy Minister of Recreation & Conservation
> Parliament Buildings
> Victoria, British Columbia V8V 1X4

c) Manitoba:

> The Minister of Tourism, Recreation & Cultural Affairs
> Legislature Building
> Winnipeg, Manitoba
> or

Historic Resources Branch
Department of Tourism, Recreation and Cultural Affairs
200 Vaughan Street
Winnipeg, Manitoba R3C 1T5

d) New Brunswick:
The Minister of Education
Legislature Building
Fredericton, New Brunswick
or
Historical Resources Administration
P.O. Box 6000
Fredericton, New Brunswick E3B 5H1

e) Newfoundland:
The Minister of Tourism
Confederation Building
St. John's, Newfoundland
or
Historic Resources Branch
Newfoundland Museum
Duckworth Street
St. John's, Newfoundland A1C 1G9

f) Nova Scotia:
The Minister of Education
Legislative Building
Halifax, Nova Scotia
or
The Director
Nova Scotia Museum
1747 Summer Street
Halifax, Nova Scotia B3H 3A6

g) Ontario:
The Minister of Culture & Recreation
Queen's Park
Toronto, Ontario
or

Ministry of Culture & Recreation
77 Bloor Stret West,
Toronto, Ontario M7A 2R9

Please note that the actual designation of cultural sites in Ontario is a municipal responsibility, not a provincial one. Furthermore, the functions of the Ministry and the quasi-governmental Ontario Heritage Foundation are often shared.

h) Prince Edward Island:
   The Minister of Environment and Tourism
   Province House
   Charlottetown, P.E.I.
         or
   P.E.I. Heritage Foundation
   2 Kent Street
   Charlottetown, Prince Edward Island C1A 7L9

i) Quebec:
   Le Ministre des Affaires culturelles
   Assemblée Nationale
   Québec, Québec
         or
   Directeur Général du Patrimoine
   Ministère des Affaires culturelles
   6, rue/Université
   Québec, Québec G1R 5A6

j) Saskatchewan:
   The Minister of Tourism and
         Renewable Resources
   Legislature Buildings
   Regina, Saskatchewan
         or
   Supervisor of Historic Resources
   Department of Culture & Youth
   2002 Victoria, 11th Floor
   Regina, Saskatchewan S4P 3V3

These are government agencies which should have an interest in this subject matter. However, in four provinces, the ultimate decision to protect a site is made not by the Minister, but by the Cabinet (upon the Minister's recommendation). Those provinces are British Columbia, Manitoba, Newfoundland and Prince Edward Island. In two provinces, Ontario and Nova Scotia, no provincial official is fully empowered to protect heritage sites.

(iii) The Municipal Level

In virtually all Canadian cities, the administration of heritage sites and areas is administered through the municipal planning department.

PUBLIC AND SEMI-PUBLIC INSTITUTIONS AND ADVISORY BOARDS

(i) The National Level

The Historic Sites and Monuments Board advises the Minister of Indian Affairs and Northern Development on the designation of "National Historic Sites". Contact:

> The Secretary
> Historic Sites & Monuments Board of Canada
> Ottawa, Ontario K1A 0H4

Another important federal advisory body is the Federal Advisory Co-ordinating Committee on Heritage Conservation (FACCHC), mentioned earlier. It can be reached care of the Department of Indian Affairs & Northern Development at the same address as above.

A governmental organization has been formed to hold annual meetings of officials responsible for heritage conservation. Those officials are both from the federal and provincial governments. The organization is named the Canadian Conference on Historical Resources; since its address changes annually, a citizen might find it more convenient to contact this body care of the heritage authorities in his own province.

(ii) The Provincial Level

Five provinces have government-sponsored "foundations" which have an interest in "cultural property". Those five provinces are Alberta, Manitoba, Ontario, Prince Edward Island and British Columbia. They are authorized both to advise governments and acquire properties

A "foundation" is sometimes thought of as a non-profit corporation which enjoys some independence from government thanks to an *endowment* . . . not surprisingly, if one looks in a dictionary. However, these five "foundations" are governmentally created, and ultimately responsible to their provincial government. Some, however, have endowment funds which supplement the funds received from the provincial budget.

The Alberta Historical Resources Foundation's head office is 121 8th Ave. S.W., Calgary, Alberta.

The British Columbia Heritage Trust can be reached care of the Department of Recreation & Conservation, at the The Parliament Buildings in Victoria.

Heritage Manitoba can be reached care of the Manitoba Historic Resources Branch, 200 Vaughan Street, Winnipeg, Manitoba.

The Ontario Heritage Foundation's address is at 77 Bloor Street West, Toronto, Ontario.

The Prince Edward Island Heritage Foundation's address is 2 Kent Street, Charlottetown, P.E.I.

In addition, most provinces have advisory boards which assist the powers that be in formulating and applying heritage policy.

(iii) The Municipal Level

Advisory boards frequently exist at the municipal level. Usually, municipalities do not even need special enabling legislation to create such bodies . . . as long as their function remains strictly advisory. Some other jurisdictions prefer to bestow upon these advisory bodies the blessing of special legislation as in the case of Ontario's Local Architectural Conservation Advisory Committees (LACACs).

CHAPTER 8

PRIVATE ASSOCIATIONS AND NON-PUBLIC RESOURCES

PRIVATE ASSOCIATIONS

(i) General

There are several hundred associations which have a direct or indirect interest in the conservation of our built environment. Some, such as the Society for the Study of Architecture and the Canadian Environmental Law Association are national in scope. The overwhelming majority of such organizations, however, are of a purely local nature. There are some one hundred and fifty groups which are members of Heritage Canada.

These groups come in all shapes and sizes. Legal status depends on whether the association has been incorporated. Once incorporated, it may apply for registration under the Canadian *Income Tax Act* as a tax-deductible charity. This registration means that any person contributing money to such an organization may deduct this contribution from his taxable income.

Despite this feature, the financial structure of most public interest groups is shaky when they must rely exclusively upon membership fees and donations. Most do not have enough money to buy a decent typewriter, let alone hire a secretary. Some are fortunate enough to obtain funding from charities or government research contracts: these contracts permit them to hire paid research staff. The vitality of most organizations, however, is dependent upon the public interest, leadership and plain old intestinal fortitude of their members.

(ii) Heritage Canada

The largest non-government organization concerned with heritage property in Canada is Heritage Canada. It is a non-profit corporation founded and incorporated in 1973 under the *Canada Corporations Act*. It has a Board of Governors elected by the 10,000 members and a full-time staff of less than twenty. Its financial base is

Citizens in Lunenburg, Nova Scotia, are conducting this restoration with the financial backing of Heritage Canada

composed of the membership fees, donations, and proceeds from a $12,000,000 fund which was deposited in trust for Heritage Canada by the federal government in 1973. Aside from the fact that Heritage Canada is legally limited in how it can invest its endowment fund, and aside from the presence of two representatives of federal ministries among Heritage Canada's fourteen governors, Heritage Canada has no budgetary or structural links with any government.

Heritage Canada does, however, have contractual links with some governments. It has a property-holding agreement with the federal government which permits it to give relatively favourable tax treatment to donors of property. It has entered into agreements with provincial governments such as the co-sponsorship of publications and films. It has also entered into agreements with municipal governments, such as a shared commitment to conservation in and with the City of Edmonton, Alberta. Aside from contractual arrangements, Heritage Canada has loose working understandings with many other governments and agencies throughout Canada.

Heritage Canada's primary duty, however, is to the non-governmental conservation movement: it acts as the focus and the voice of conservationists from coast to coast.

The programs conducted by Heritage Canada have also dealt with more than words, i.e. such things as loans to member groups conducting non-profit renovation projects. It has been concluded that the most can be done with available funds by promoting the protection and renovation of heritage *neighbourhoods*. This conclusion was reached after considerable study of the internal economic dynamics of such areas and led to a wide-ranging economic and promotional program loosely called the "area conservation program".

Heritage Canada's investment in such areas first took the form of feasibility studies for wide-scale renovation. If the studies were affirmative, and if local co-operation (governmental and private) was indicative of a potential catalytic effect for further investment, then Heritage Canada would purchase and renovate properties with the intention of resale and reinvestment in further renovations. Such purchase, sale and reinvestment is sometimes called a "revolving fund", and has been used successfully in other jurisdictions, such as the U.S. and the U.K. Heritage Canada would also promote the establishment of a permanent local foundation to guarantee the continued administration of renovations in that community.

The publications of Heritage Canada bring the membership up-to-date with recent developments in conservation efforts as well as the conclusions of research. Annexed to the publications component is the media component, which promotes the message of heritage conservation through written and electronic media. Written materials are sometimes printed as specialized publications, but most information is published in a bi-monthly magazine, *Heritage Canada* which is sent free to all members.

Edmonton's Strathcona district. This is one of several heritage areas in which Heritage Canada is co-operating with municipal authorities in renovation efforts.

Many members joined Heritage Canada through a regional or local heritage organization. Heritage Canada sponsors meetings among these organizations, in the form of "regional councils". The primary purpose of these councils is the exchange of information not only among the various groups but also with Heritage Canada, so that the Ottawa office may be better attuned to the needs and aspirations of that particular region and formulate its approaches accordingly. In addition, there is a general meeting of the membership once per year.

Research is carried on at the Ottawa office and is also contracted out. The work conducted at the office is almost exclusively on the subjects of law, economics, finance and taxation. Work contracted is almost exclusively on the subjects of education and of urban planning for proposed heritage conservation areas. Virtually no historical research is done except insofar as it is necessary for an urban plan. Instead, a fairly clear-cut division of labour has emerged: the member groups research *what* to save and *why* to save it, whereas Heritage Canada researches *how* to save it; the parties advise each other accordingly.

Part of the research function since 1973 has been to identify the problem areas of heritage conservation, and to devise the most appropriate means of solution. The legal research leads primarily to legislative recommendations and legal advice to governments and conservationists. Tax research leads exclusively to legislative recommendations. Economic, financial and planning research lead to legislative recommendations, to private programs conducted by Heritage Canada and to information for member groups, developers, etc.

PHILANTHROPIC AND NON-PROFIT FUNDS

There is little which would delight conservationists more than free money (no surprise there). However, there is no large private philanthropic organization in Canada devoted exclusively to the financing of renovations or restorations.

There are some large foundations, such as the Devonian Foundation in Alberta or the Macdonald-Stewart Foundation in Quebec, which will invest directly in heritage projects. For example, Devonian has budgeted millions for the improvement of the appearance of small Alberta towns. However, most such organizations will invest *indirectly:* they will donate sums to a registered charitable heritage organization to carry out the work.

REVENUE-PRODUCING FUNDS

(i) General

When there is no free money for a project, people often look for not-so-free money, i.e. from banks, trust companies, insurance companies, finance companies and other lenders.

It is probable that finance companies and other lenders could be persuaded to make loans for renovations on heritage structures: but these lenders are accustomed to dealing with relatively higher risks, and rates of interest are usually too high to permit the project to be profitable.

In order for a project to be viable, it is usually imperative to obtain a mortgage loan from a bank, trust company or insurance company. These institutions, however, are relatively conservative; and co-operation with renovation projects has been impeded by a number of factors which have often led to a refusal of the loan application. One entrepreneur claims to have obtained more favourable financial arrangements for his recycling project from the *mafia*. The hang-ups of more "conventional" lenders are described in the following sections.

(ii) The Income Tax Act

As detailed later, a loophole in the *Income Tax Act* permits those who demolish structures to avoid taxes. Furthermore, another inconsistency in the Act makes proper renovation less advantageous than other kinds of expenditures.

Financial institutions are aware of this, and hence they often look upon renovation as a second-best use of the property. This in turn means that at best, the institution will have doubts about the business acumen of the loan applicant; at worst, they will think he's nuts. This problem can only be solved by amendments to the *Income Tax Act* which conservationists are seeking.

(iii) The Choice of Architect

The actual physical cost of renovation is another inhibiting factor. Many Canadian architects are not equipped with the expertise to work effectively with older buildings. The choice of architects to handle renovation work can often decide whether a given project will be incredibly profitable or a financial disaster. Unless a lender has some grasp of this phenomenon, he will not be able to assess the risk factor of the loan, and shall refuse it accordingly.

In an attempt to solve this problem, Heritage Canada is compiling a list of architects who have worked in renovation projects.

(iv) Insurability

Mortgage loans are automatically refused if it is impossible to obtain a policy insuring the premises for the benefit of the lender. Some conservationists have claimed that insurance companies are refusing to insure some older areas of Canadian cities, thus making it impossible to obtain financing for renovation and thereby accelerating deterioration.

The claim has certainly proved true in the United States, where this discrimination (called "redlining") by insurance and finance companies was so widespread that it provoked corrective legislation. It has been argued, however, that the "insurability problem" in Canada is more the result of misunderstanding of Canadian insurance practices than an inherent weakness in those practices. Indeed, some argue that once government gives a strong commitment to heritage conservation in an area, the insurability problem disappears by itself;

this is allegedly the case, for example, in St. John's Newfoundland. In view of the various claims being made, Heritage Canada is currently conducting research to clarify this situation.

(v) Appraisal

Some entrepreneurs have claimed that the largest single obstacle facing loans for renovations is that Canadian financial institutions do not know how to appraise older buildings, nor do they know how to appraise renovation projects. No single financial institution in Canada has allegedly seen enough of these projects to say that it has any understanding of the economic dynamics or the risk involved.

Unlike American banks, which will hire outside experts in renovation projects to assess the viability of a mortgage loan application for such a project, Canadian institutions tend to rely upon their own personnel. Since there is little experience of renovation projects in Canada, that personnel cannot assess the profitability of the proposed renovation project; and since they cannot assess it, the application for a mortgage loan is often refused unless the borrower has so much personal wealth that he didn't need the money in the first place.

Disgruntled entrepreneurs summarize the scenario like this: since the institutions have little experience, they refuse loans; and since they refuse loans, they acquire little experience. Under such circumstances, it is difficult to finance even the most profitable renovation projects.

This problem is diminishing in some centres such as Toronto and Vancouver where the viability of recycling buildings is increasingly apparent; but even in those cities it still causes concern. In order to break this vicious circle, it is necessary to give the institutions sufficient knowledge of such projects in order to recognize safe risks and to lend accordingly. This can be done in two ways, described below.

(iv) The Path Toward a Solution

The first task is to educate the appraisers working for the financial institutions. This is a task which Heritage Canada has been attempting to undertake in collaboration with the Appraisal Institute of Canada. Heritage Canada has also undertaken an inventory of successful recycling projects, in the hope that the experience gained could be placed at the disposal of both architects and appraisers.

Another suggestion of the entrepreneurs was the controversial system called "mortgage guarantees".

Under this proposal, an institution (entrepreneurs suggested Central Mortgage & Housing Corporation or Heritage Canada) would *guarantee* the repayment of mortgage loans to renovation projects when the *age* of the structure makes conventional financing impossible. Upon default, the institution would repay the loan and acquire title to the property; but since only a small minority of loans would presumably default, the institution would succeed in sponsoring renovation expenditures far in excess of what it was actually spending on the program.

The financial community's response to this proposal has been contradictory. Almost all financiers agreed that they commiserated with the plight of heritage buildings, but that they nonetheless were very suspicious of any tinkering with the status quo. One financier said that a mortgage guarantee system would not finance a single building in addition to those being financed under current practices; another said the reverse, i.e. that a guarantee system would precipitate a rash of loans on irresponsible projects. In view of this perplexing response from those most knowledgeable in the subject, conservationists have had to put their thinking caps back on to scrutinize the subject further.

In the meantime, some conservationists have urged Central Mortgage & Housing Corporation to look into the possibility of guaranteeing mortgages.

This federal agency already guarantees many kinds of loans, and promotes the renovation of dwellings. Unfortunately, the *National Housing Act* which specifies the C.M.H.C.'s powers does not permit it to guarantee renovations of commercial properties . . . not even when the building is being converted to residential use. This unfortunate situation will hopefully change (at least for residences) in the near future, when the *National Housing Act* comes up for review.

For the time being, conservationists can only hope that further research will uncover a solution to the financial problem. Obviously, if the economics of renovation were radically improved (e.g. by tax reforms), financial institutions would respond favourably; if mortgage guarantees are eventually found to be viable, that scheme may be adopted; and if sufficient documentary evidence is presented to financiers concerning the viability of recycling, prevailing attitudes may change. Conservationists must work on all these fronts, and are also trying to establish a better general rapport with the financial community. It is hoped that sooner or later, financial institutions will have acquired sufficient knowledge and experience in renovation to make intelligent loans to viable renovation projects without the necessity of guarantees or other financial commitments from any institution. To date, the financial community has proved particularly difficult to seduce; but conservationists are confident that sooner or later the merit of their cause will be seen and the courtship will be consummated.

PART IV
THE GOVERNMENTS' FINAN-CIAL TECHNIQUES

CHAPTER 9

PURCHASE

PURCHASE OF PROPERTY RIGHTS

(i) Scope

The Canadian federal government, provinces, local authorities and other institutions and associations have, from time to time, allocated funds to purchase sites and to restore them. The total amount being spent has never been calculated.

(ii) Intent

There are some Canadians who appear under the impression that if any building is to be saved, the government should purchase it. When asked what the government will then do with the structure, their response is a conditioned reflex reminiscent of Pavlov's dogs: "Turn it into a community cultural centre or local museum".

If every meritorious structure were "saved" in this way, we would soon have more cultural centres than hockey rinks and maple groves. That could do strange things to the Canadian self-image.

There are tens of thousands of worthy heritage structures in Canada. As much as we may like museums and cultural centres, we simply do not need tens of thousands of them. UNESCO Recommendations have stated that heritage buildings should, as much as possible, continue to serve a function within the economic life of the community. In any event, there is simply no way Canadian taxpayers could support the purchase of every meritorious site; the Canadian economy would be in an even stranger situation than it is now.

Governmental purchase should therefore be viewed only as a last resort, when no other viable use can be made of a structure. When a viable use exists, the proprietors should be encouraged to put the property to such use, and the government's financial responsibility should be limited to any unduly excessive costs which might be imposed by preservation and renovation.

PURCHASE OF LESSER INTERESTS

(i) The Mechanism

It is possible, under both the Civil Law system of Quebec and the Common Law systems of the other provinces, to acquire real interests in property less than full ownership.

Under the Civil Law system of Quebec, a legal mechanism with the misleadingly sinister title of "personal servitude" can bind an owner (and all his successors) to refrain from doing something on his property, such as altering it or tearing down buildings. This contract can be signed by the owner with any other person or corporation; Heritage Canada has entered into such an agreement with a proprietor who binds himself not to alter or demolish his property without Heritage Canada's consent.

Similar agreements are possible in the Common Law provinces under the name of "restrictive covenants", but the Common Law imposes a condition: if the contract is to bind future owners, the party with whom the owner contracts must also own land which is directly benefitted by the contract.

Most conservationists and groups were not able to meet that condition. Consequently, six provinces (Ontario, P.E.I., British Columbia, Alberta, New Brunswick and Newfoundland) amended their legislation so that restrictive covenants could protect heritage

The Lebel House in Aylmer Quebec, currently being used as Restaurant Le Vicomte, is the object of a conservation agreement with Heritage Canada, the first agreement of its kind in Canada.

property even if no other land benefitted. In the case of the last three provinces, such easements and covenants could even be signed by a proprietor with a group which was not a government or agency. Several other provinces are considering amendments which would follow these examples.

There are two primary features which distinguish these mechanisms from the designation procedure of statutes. The first is that once the agreement is signed, protection does not necessarily depend upon the government: the decision-maker can be a foundation, or even any person at all (in Quebec). The second feature is that it is purely contractual: it cannot be imposed without the owner's consent.

(ii) Acquisition

The fact that the owner's consent is obligatory means that the agreement is attributable either to philanthropy or to remuneration.

It would, of course, be nice if all kinds of owners of heritage structures came forward to freely offer their signature for such agreements. The prospect is unlikely. Quebec operated a similar scheme between 1921 and 1963; it gave the scheme forty-two years to work, and finally realized that results were negligeable.

There is, of course, a remarkable hybrid composed of both public spirit and looking-out-for-number-one: it is called enlightened self-interest. Conservationists in the U.K. and the U.S.A. have had considerable success in persuading owners that it was in their long-term interest to sign such agreements without further remuneration. In 1975, the Ontario Heritage Foundation set out to drum up support for such agreements, and its program now appears to be rolling along smoothly. This is no mean tribute to the skill and diplomacy of the O.H.F.'s negotiators.

The sad but inescapable fact remains that many owners will not sign until they are remunerated. Heritage Canada has been researching ways of doing this indirectly through the *Income Tax Act;* in the meantime, some government agencies have been dealing in cash, although they prefer to think of such transactions as "grants" rather than "payments".

A number of Canadian conservationists have followed the lead of some Americans in declaring that such agreements are the *panacea* of the conservation movement. The agreements are unquestionably useful; but if the main thrust of conservation becomes contingent upon the owners' approval, then many worthy buildings will be lost. Furthermore, if the main thrust of conservation also becomes contingent upon remuneration, then our resources will be exhausted before we have barely begun to save our heritage. Consequently, the acquisition of these interests should be viewed in the same light as the purchase of full ownership: they are useful tools which may come in handy in all sorts of situations, but they should not distract conservationists from the fact that as far as most experienced governments are concerned, proper *legislative* controls remain the primary guarantor of heritage conservation.

CHAPTER 10

THE TAXMAN COMETH

THE FEDERAL LEVEL

Anyone who believes that Canada's only two official languages are English and French has never read the *Income Tax Act.*

The problem is not peculiar to Canada: taxation questions have been giving migraines to conservationists in a host of countries. Accordingly, various UNESCO Recommendations have called upon member states to use their tax system to deter demolition and promote renovation.

Canada, being the good member of the international community that it is, voted for these Recommendations; however, when conservationists started scrutinizing the realities of the Canadian *Income Tax Act*, they learned that it did precisely the reverse: it promoted demolition and failed to promote renovation.

This situation appears to have come about quite by accident. The tax treatment of buildings has changed relatively little over the past thirty years; it is extremely unlikely that those who drafted it could forsee its effects on heritage. It is equally unlikely that the Department of National Revenue, in all the turmoil which followed Tax Reform six years ago, could have had the time to analyse the long-term effects of tax provisions which had seemed so innocuous for over thirty years.It is only recently that it has been discovered that the *Income Tax Act's* effects on heritage are not innocuous at all. Those effects are as follows.

The Income Tax Act says that buildings are not demolished, but instead get "lost", as if they flew away and nested elsewhere

(i) Demolition

While rummaging through the Act, conservationists came upon a curious feature of the obscure definitions section of the statute: demolition is not a "disposition" of property. This is the only case in which an owner can dispose of a property without having "disposed of it", for the purposes of the Act.

This oversight is very convenient for speculators who have been avoiding tax by claiming depreciation in excess of the real market depreciation of the property. It is upon "disposition" that federal officials can check whether the property has been overdepreciated (and income tax avoided accordingly); but since demolition is not a disposition, there is no way of checking for this tax avoidance.

Downtown Canada: the ubiquitous parking lot is frequently the result of tax incentives rather than pure market pressure

Another consequence of this oversight is not only costly to the public treasury, it is downright weird.

We know that according to the Act, a demolished building has not been disposed of, but where has it gone? The poor thing has disappeared. According to the *Income Tax Act*, it got "lost", as if it had flown away and nested elsewhere.

Every time our friendly neighbourhood speculator invests in a building and demolishes it, he can report the building as "lost" on his income tax return. This "terminal loss", equal to the book value of the building, is entirely deductible from his taxable income.

The cumulative effect of these two advantages is this: after going through all the horrors of calculating capital gains and other creatures, it has been estimated that an owner who demolishes a building in which he had invested can avoid paying taxes on a sum equal to *half the book value of the building at time of purchase.* For example, if the building was worth $100,000 at the time of purchase, demolition will ultimately represent a saving of taxes on $50,000 worth of income.

That is the extent to which the public treasury, i.e. all the taxpayers of Canada, are subsidizing the destruction of their own structural heritage. No one knows how much the total subsidy in Canada amounts to: it may be tens of millions of dollars, or even hundreds of millions.

This subsidy, along with the advantage which municipal taxation attaches to demolition (described later), are probably the greatest reason why downtown Canada often looks as if it was blitzed. Winnipeg, for example, has been turned into one of North America's largest day-care centres for automobiles: it has been estimated that about 60% of private land in its central core area is covered by parking lots.

In view of this harsh economic reality, it becomes obvious that the efforts of planners, from the heights of the Ministry of State for Urban Affairs down to benighted conservation groups, to make our urban cores livable have been so much whistling in the dark.

Now that this problem has been identified, conservationists are eager to find a solution. That is no picnic. As sympathetic as tax officials may be, they are not at liberty to turn the *Income Tax Act* upside down: this incentive to demolition has been built into the tax system for thirty years, and cannot be removed without making fundamental adjustments to the system.

This is more difficult than it appears. Although *hundreds* of amendments to the *Income Tax Act* are passed annually, some are more fundamental than others; the incentive to demolition can be removed only when a thorough analysis is made of all the repercussions. Fortunately, this analysis is currently under way.

(ii) Renovation

What does the *Income Tax Act* do to promote renovation? The answer is simple: nothing.

Again, this problem is not based upon the malevolence of some unseen bureaucrat: renovations have simply not been an issue of such national importance that they have been given special treatment in the Act. It should be remembered that an issue must be of profound importance before it obtains special treatment, i.e. distracts tax officials from their basic duty of raising revenue.

Although renovations to heritage buildings may not have qualified for such treatment in the past, there are certain features which now deserve a fresh examination.

If a heritage building is to be retained on a site, it must often compete economically with the prospect of new construction on that same site. This, according to some conservationists, is where the *Income Tax Act* is less than fair: it gives a significant advantage to new construction.

A special loophole has been built into the Act so that developers can claim tax-deductible losses even when they are making profits: this exceptional provision, called the MURB provision (for Multiple Unit Residential Buildings), permits the developer to claim tax-deductible depreciation in excess of the revenue on the project. That revenue not only becomes *tax free*, but the excess in depreciation permits the developer to claim a tax deductible *loss* which he can use to render *other income tax free*. This is called a "tax shelter". Although the federal government attempted to close this "shelter" some time ago, complaints from the real estate industry resulted in the shelter being reopened.

Consequently, the developer who demolishes a structure receives special tax treatment not only for the demolition, but also for the apartment or townhouse which will be built upon the site.

Renovation not only fails to receive any comparable tax incentives, but even fails to obtain a tax treatment consistent with basic tax principles. This is particularly true of renovation of buildings designated under a heritage statute; to understand the problem, one must again plunge into some of the niceties of the *Income Tax Act*.

When one invests in a building, work on the building can fall into one of two categories: expenditures made "once and for all", and those made for a limited time only. Expenditures made *"once and for all"* are called "capital expenditures", and are *not tax-deductible*; expenditures made for a *limited time* (e.g. maintenance, regular replacement of worn-out parts, etc.) are called "business expenditures", and are entirely *tax-deductible*. Obviously, the proprietor is in a more favourable tax position if his work on a building is treated as a business expense, i.e. *not* made "once and for all".

The Department of National Revenue usually treats renovations as being made "once and for all", and so they are *not tax-deductible* even in the case of buildings which have been *governmentally designated as heritage sites*. This policy, which is relatively unusual in the western world, leads to a legal contradiction. The legislative intent of various provincial heritage statutes is clearly to promote the retention of certain specified heritage buildings *indefinitely*; in that context, *no* expenditure on such buildings can be *legally* treated as being reliably made *"once and for all"*. Consequently, the approach taken by the Department of National Revenue to renovation expenses *contradicts the intent of the heritage statutes*.

This is not altogether surprising: the tax system in question could not have made a special provision for heritage statutes because it came into existence before they did. However, now that this incongruity has been identified, it is hoped that it will be resolved for the benefit both of consistency and of heritage. No one claims that the solution will be either quick or easy: it involves tax questions which are every bit as complex as the issues in the demolition problem. Nevertheless, the question is currently under study and conservationists are optimistic of an eventual solution.

THE PROVINCIAL LEVEL

Only one province, Quebec, has formalized a system of tax cuts for classified heritage properties. It states that the evaluation on which *municipal* taxation is computed can be lowered by as much as 50% on non-commercial premises

THE MUNICIPAL LEVEL

(i) General

In all provinces except Newfoundland, municipal revenue is collected in an age-old way: all properties are evaluated in the perspective of their market value, and then a certain percentage of that assessment becomes payable in municipal taxes. In Newfoundland, the system is highly similar, except that evaluation is directed toward *rental* value rather than *market* value.

The evaluation of properties for tax purposes is an intriguing process. The theory of appraisal in Canada has been refined extensively. Its primary criterion, "highest and best use", has developed into a sophisticated doctrine encompassing many variables beyond what

Anyone familiar with appraisals for tax purposes will know that renovation adds more than charm to a building

were once called the three pillars of appraisal: location, location and location.

On the other hand, the technique of some "appraisers" is no more complicated than looking at the value of the property next door.

Into this structure of municipal finance have been injected politicians, merchants, conservationists, appraisers and others. The results have been some very strange debates, particularly in proposed heritage areas. The politicians want to increase the tax base so that municipal revenues will rise, but are occasionally worried about population displacement. Merchants' groups sometimes want population to be displaced to make way for commercial uses. Conservationists want population stability, would like to see more municipal expenditures on services, but want to lower or at least freeze taxes in the area. The outcome of these competing interests has frequently been like a Russian novel: the multitudinous characters assemble and stagnate together.

(ii) The Conflicting Interests

If municipal governments are requested to improve services in an area (street lighting, sidewalks, benches, etc.) then they usually expect to see an increase in property values which will be translated into increased municipal revenue to pay back their costs.

Conservationists occasionally get miffed at this demand, because it is often directed at heritage projects but seldom at demolition and redevelopment schemes. In principle, however, the demand appears perfectly reasonable. Conservationists have been able to reply with figures indicating marked increases in property values for heritage areas which have been the subject of protection and renovation activity. For example, Vancouver's Gastown saw an increase of 81% in six years.

This does not, however, help the owner of a heritage property in the area. The more he improves and renovates his property, the more he is taxed; indeed, since he is helping the *entire area* become more picturesque and

153

fashionable (thus increasing the value of his *land* as well as his building), it is conceivable that his evaluation for *tax* purposes might increase at an even *higher rate than the value of his improvements*.

This is no incentive for renovation; but in most nonresidential areas (with the exception of some rare cases such as Toronto) these extra costs can be passed on without causing major dislocations.

In residential areas, however, the effect of increased taxes can be disastrous. Increased taxes mean increased rents and housing costs, frequently to those who can least afford them; and many precedents throughout North America have indicated that neighborhood dislocation and social hardship can result.

Conservationists in residential areas must therefore argue that revenues to pay back governmental expenditures can be derived in other ways, aside from increasing municipal taxation on the area. Again, precedents are fortunately on the side of conservationists. Other heritage areas have invariably demonstrated a substantial increase in tourist spending. Thanks to sales taxes and economic conditions generally, this increased economic activity sooner or later is reflected in municipal budgets. The City of Quebec is a good example: its heritage character is sufficiently attractive that 35% of the city's economy is based upon tourism.

This phenomenon, however, also creates pressures for population displacement. People who try to cash in on increased tourism lobby municipal governments to permit more and more restaurants, bars and night clubs to encroach upon residential areas. If the population is not priced out of the area, it can be driven out by noise, fumes and drunks. In the words of one Quebec conservationist, "this city is becoming Canada's Disneyland; it's a nice place to visit, but who wants to live in Disneyland?".

(iii) Dealing with the Problem

If the needs of municipal finance and population stability are both to be met by heritage conservation programs, it will be necessary to perform something of a balancing act.

It should be possible to find ways of raising revenue through tourism, and thus to avoid (as much as possible) increased taxes upon renovated heritage structures. At the very least, there should be a moratorium upon assessment increases for a specified period. Particular effort should be made to avoid tax increases in residential areas. At the same time, a conscious policy must be adopted to prevent undue encroachment upon residences by other uses. In short, conservationists who advocate municipal action can rely on no substitute for homework, and lots of it.

CHAPTER 11

COST SHARING AND OTHER FINAN-CIAL HELP

GENERAL

> For those who enjoy the challenge of the unknown, and who are too old to qualify for the crew of an orbiting space station, renovating the house is certainly fulfilling.
>
> Eric Nicol

Despite these auspicious words, the subject of financial assistance to renovation is not a romantic one. It often appears that the only people who are interested in ways of obtaining money for renovations are usually people who are looking for money for renovations . . . for whom the subject suddenly acquires passionate interest.

For the rest of us plebs, the esoteric subject of financial aid to renovation projects may appear rather forbidding. It becomes all the more forbidding when one learns that by the time one has figured out the maze of programs, that is precisely the moment officialdom is likely to change the system. It is one of life's mysteries that groups such as the Canadian Association of Housing and Renewal Officers do not display a higher incidence of nervous breakdowns.

The instant obsolescence of information is the principal reason why so little has been published on the subject of financial aid to renovation projects. Some provinces are even reluctant to issue brochures explaining their own programs. It would be equally futile to attempt a proper inventory of such programs in this text; the best that can be attempted on this kaleidoscopic canvas are a few broad brush strokes.

THE FEDERAL LEVEL

(i) Introduction
There are two ways that the federal government enters into cost-sharing arrangements. The first is by direct subsidy. The second is by entering into agreements with other levels of government whereby the federal government transfers funds but the other governments carry on the administration of the subsidy program.

(ii) Historic Sites
The only direct federal funding program for "historic" sites is the one administered by the Department of Indian Affairs and Northern Development for sites "marked or commemorated" as being of national significance under the federal *Historic Sites & Monuments Act.* Treasury Board Minute 623840 states:

(1) where title to the historic property is vested in Her Majesty in right of Canada;

(2) where title to the historic property is vested in the name of the other party to the agreement;

(3) where title to the historic property is to become vested in the other party to the agreement.

Regulations

(a) when condition (1) prevails, the federal government share should be not in excess of 75% of the costs of restoration;

(b) when condition (2) prevails, the federal government share should be not in excess of 50% of the costs of acquisition and 50% of the costs of restoration.

Officials have succeeded in unravelling this tortured prose, and make subsidies available accordingly. Interested parties should write to the Historic Sites Monuments Board in Ottawa, Ontario K1A 0H4.

The minister and his advisors, however, are decidedly selective in the sites they choose to subsidize. They have traditionally developed very cold feet when dealing with cemeteries or with churches in active use; although there are some signs of a warming trend, conservationists must still expect only a few select sites to pass the rigorous federal screening process, which can take six months.

A more sweeping cost-sharing program has been in the works for some time. Heritage Canada suggested a joint federal-provincial funding program in 1974, and negotiations were launched to set up a "Canadian Register of Heritage Property", i.e. a list of worthy buildings (perhaps 5000?) which would be eligible for subsidies. After multitudinous meetings and the obligatory wailing and gnashing of teeth which accompanies every federal-provincial shared-cost program, the Minister of Indian and Northern Affairs announced, on February 23, 1976, that the "Canadian Register of Heritage Property" had been agreed upon and would proceed imminently.

Conservationists who held their breath are in deep trouble. Ottawa pundits do not currently predict the establishment of such a program before 1979, at the earliest.

(iii) CMHC Improvement Programs

Central Mortgage and Housing Corporation is the federal government's trump card in the urban affairs game. There was a time when the urban renewal bulldozer could be considered CMHC's mascot; but times have changed, and the agency is now heavily involved in promoting the renovation of housing stock. This work is not aimed at promoting "Heritage", but simply at renovating structures so as to provide adequate housing, regardless of architectural or historic features.

Over the past few years, CMHC has used two major programs for that purpose: the Neighbourhood Improvement Program (NIP) and the Residential Rehabilitation Assistance Program (RRAP). The first, NIP, was aimed at developing plans and amenities for neighborhoods which risked becoming run-down. The area had to be a) predominantly residential; b) in need of rehabilitation; c) have low to moderate income residents, and d) have inadequate social and recreational amenities. The NIP program provided grants and loans to assist 1) planning costs and administration for the area; 2) acquisition and development of land for amenities and housing; 3) development of maintenance standards to be enforced in the area; 4) certain loans to commercial premises, and 5) relocation of any displaced residents.

NIP areas were eligible for the Residential Rehabilitation Assistance Program (RRAP); or in the words of those who administered these programs, "once the area has been nipped it can also be rrapped". RRAP provided low-interest loans (partly forgivable) to residents of the area for renovations.

These programs elicited an enormous response: communities from all over Canada jostled one another to set up NIP and RRAP projects within their boundaries. The demand for NIP and RRAP became almost embarrassing.

NIP and RRAP, however, were experimental. By the end of 1977, the Ottawa cocktail party circuit was humming with conservationists and housing pundits speculating about the future of such programs. The prevailing theory was the one which probably appeared the most implausible to anyone unacquainted with the bureaucratic mind: NIP and RRAP were in deep trouble because according to some officials, they were in such great demand that something had to be wrong with them.

Admittedly, NIP and RRAP had had some lumps and bumps. Some critics complained that too much money was finding its way into curling rinks and sewer systems; others said that the conditions for eligibility were too strict . . . or too loose. RRAP marches on; but on March 31st, 1978, the late NIP expired.

It was gone, but not forgotten! Plans were undertaken to launch a son-of-NIP. For further details as to how

these plans have unfolded, contact:
> Central Mortgage & Housing Corp.
> Montreal Road,
> Ottawa, Ontario K1A 0P7.

PROVINCIAL AND MUNICIPAL PROGRAMS

Some provincial and municipal subsidy programs are specifically aimed at "heritage" sites; like the federal government, however, most funding is aimed at the renovation of housing stock, regardless of architectural or historic features. Additionally, some provinces have developed fairly elaborate programs to fund the rehabilitation of commercial areas. As usual, these programs are in such a constant state of flux that they can be outlined only in general terms.

Several provinces have financial schemes to subsidize renovations to heritage sites which have been designated for protection by the provincial government. Quebec has the most elaborate set of rules to provide financial aid; the systems in Alberta and Saskatchewan are also well-defined. In most of the other provinces, subsidies tend to be determined on a more discretionary and *ad hoc* basis.

It is extremely rare for government funding for renovations on private property to exceed 50% of the cost of those renovations, and there is usually an upper limit on the expenditures to be subsidized. Further information on these various programs is available from the authorities responsible for heritage conservation in each province.

In almost every case, financial assistance is contingent upon *renovations* being conducted; the one major exception to that rule is British Columbia. That province's *Heritage Conservation Act* forces the province to turn cash over to the owners of designated heritage property if there has been a decrease in the property's value; that obligation is binding, whether the owner undertakes any repairs or not. Furthermore, when a

160

"Bad news, Ethel . . . our Heritage Building designation has been reconsidered . . . ."

No joke: the very thought of paying compensation has forced Vancouver to limit its heritage designations. The first casualty was Vancouver's oldest surviving school (below), destroyed by a provincial agency.

municipality designates a heritage building for protection, the *Heritage Conservation Act* makes oblique references to "compensation"; although many lawyers feel that the municipality is under no *legal obligation* to pay the owner of the property, that did not stop school trustees from threatening the City of Vancouver with a multi-million dollar lawsuit if the City designated Vancouver's oldest standing school for protection. The fact that the City backed down from designation proves that this worthy goal of financial assistance to heritage properties has been turned into a deterrent to the protection of the province's heritage.

The regulations in some other provinces lead those authorities precariously close to the same trap. The Alberta government, for example, currently has a self-imposed policy of committing itself to subsidies *every* time that it classifies a heritage site for protection; this necessarily means that the province's appraisal of its own historical resources becomes contingent upon Alberta Culture's budget, and the designation program must exhibit a selectivity which is rare in European counterparts. The U.K., for instance, has approximately one protected heritage building for every hundred inhabitants; if Alberta wished to have a comparable ratio, it would either have to amend its policy or make $300 million available to renovation projects. Even Canada's answer to Texas would balk at that kind of outlay.

The meaning of this dilemma has not been lost upon conservationists in other provinces, who have applauded the determination of Alberta and British Columbia to put their money where their mouth is, but who are nervous about getting roped into inflexible cash commitments. Consequently, many look forward to the day when financial aid to the owners of heritage buildings will come in the form of tax incentives (which do not appear in the provincial budget) rather than subsidies or other payments; there are noises in Ottawa to the effect that such tax incentives are under study. In the meantime, most provincial governments are quite content to budget funds for heritage projects while retaining deliberately vague parameters.

Housing programs are a different story.

Many provinces not only participate in CMHC's NIP and RRAP programs, but also kick in some extra programs of their own to renovate older housing stock. These programs change regularly; however, they can be broken down into several main categories.

Some provinces have programs similar to *NIP* and *RRAP*; Ontario is an example, with its *Ontario Home Renewal Program*, usually called *OHRP* and pronounced in a mildly offensive manner. Quebec also has a *"Provincial-Municipal Rehabilitation Subsidy"*; similar terms are found in New Brunswick's *Home Improvement Loans* and the *Saskatchewan Residential Rehabilitation Program*. In some other provinces, however, the program is reserved for "emergency repairs" (as in Nova Scotia's *Emergency Home Repair Program* and Manitoba's *Critical Home Repair Program*). In still other provinces, the only people eligible for subsidies or favourable loans under the special provincial initiatives are welfare recipients (as in Newfoundland's system) or senior citizens (as in Alberta's *Senior Citizen Home Improvement Program*; Saskatchewan also has such a program in addition to its other programs).

Certain provincial programs are aimed at very specific forms of renovation. British Columbia's *"Conversion Loans"* are available only for the subdivision of large old buildings into smaller units. Another program administered by the Ontario Ministry of the Environment will help an owner kick the termites out of his building. Insulation is still a further area in which subsidies are usually available: the *Canadian Home Insulation Program (CHIP)* provides funding *of some description* to most of the country for the insulation of dwellings, even though the program has been extensively altered in various provinces to suit local conditions.

The programs mentioned above are directed toward the renovation of *residential* buildings. Some provincial programs, however, are directed toward *commercial areas.*

For example, Saskatchewan's Department of Industry and Commerce launched an experimental *Main Street Development Pilot Project* to renovate the commercial cores of smaller communities. Ontario's *Downtown Revitalization Program* is far more ambitious, representing a four-year commitment totalling $40 million. The difficulty with such programs is that they almost never specify that heritage conservation should be taken into account: more taxpayers' money has been spent "revitalizing" commercial areas by obliterating their heritage aspects than by promoting such characteristics. Nevertheless, conservationists hope that the money in these programs will soon be directed toward revitalization in a manner which best displays the heritage of the community.

Finally, some cities have established financial programs specifically for heritage conservation districts within their boundaries. Montreal was probably the first; more recently, cities such as Edmonton, Winnipeg and St. John's have committed substantial sums to their heritage areas. In most of these cases, however, most money has been allotted to projects on city property rather than subsidies to private proprietors.

One aspect of financial assistance which has been mentioned earlier in passing is tax incentives. As mentioned earlier, Quebec currently provides municipal tax cuts to the owners of designated non-commercial heritage buildings. The city of Victoria introduced a similar system.

Several cities are currently studying a scheme which might be equally useful to owners of heritage property when renovation is being considered. Under this scheme, which is specifically provided for in laws such as the Quebec *Cities and Towns Act,* and which has been applied to several American cities, the value of a heritage building *for municipal tax purposes* would be frozen for a number of years: consequently, improvements to the building would not lead to a rise in municipal assessment and a proportionate rise in municipal taxes. At the end of the period (e.g five years after the renovations), methods of appraisal and taxation would return to customary levels. In this way, the municipality would defer increases in taxation until after the critical first years of a renovation project, and hopefully reap the eventual benefits which widespread renovation would bring to the municipal tax base.

As usual, there is great misery in trying to obtain any published information on the various programs which are being cooked up to promote renovation. Anyone who wishes to obtain data on programs in this area should write to the provincial authorities responsible for housing; he may also write to municipal authorities, although he should not be too surprised to find that most municipalities in Canada have not gotten any effective programs off the ground yet. Further information on specialized subjects such as insulation can be obtained from special agencies assigned for that purpose.

Information on renovation programs for commercial areas is usually available from the provincial department responsible for commerce generally. Additionally, conservationists should contact their local chambers of commerce and service clubs to learn of possible avenues of co-operation to obtain funding for renovation projects in commercial areas. This form of co-operation can often lead to very fruitful results; as a public relations gesture, the Norwich Union Insurance Company has documented some notable examples of renovation initiatives in formerly run-down commercial areas, and the company's organizational advice has become a valuable asset to many communities (even though it is a far cry from the company's business, i.e. selling life insurance!).

Canada is still far behind many European countries in funding renovation. For example, the 1971 Dutch *Decree on Financial Support for Rehabilitation* ends up by providing two thirds of the funding for renovations to privately-owned heritage buildings ... of which there are almost 40,000. Nevertheless, Canadian conservationists hope that by skillfully adapting programs to the needs of conservation in Canada, funding will be made available on a scale which will not be shamefully behind that of other civilized countries. In the meantime, we are doing our best to grin and bear A.M. Curry's dictum, "it's amazing how far money doesn't go."

PART V
SPREADING THE WORD

CHAPTER 12

THE PUBLIC

EDUCATIONAL INSTITUTIONS

(i) Elementary and Secondary Schools

The comprehensive dissemination of heritage-oriented information in Canadian elementary and secondary schools is still at the planning stage; but the task has begun, particularly as seen in school efforts to honour "Heritage Day" (described later).

(ii) College and University Levels

Many colleges and universities offer courses on heritage structures. These courses are usually non-credit: they do not count for the purposes of obtaining a degree. In some cases, however, these courses have more status. Well established diploma programs are offered at:

University of Calgary, Alberta
(Faculty of Environmental Design)
Algonquin College, Ottawa, Ontario
St. Lawrence College, Brockville, Ontario
Université Laval, Québec, Québec

GROUPS

(i) Citizens' Groups

Citizens' groups are the backbone of the Canadian heritage movement. Their incorporation, tax registration and methods of association(e.g. in Heritage Canada regional councils) were described earlier.

Most of these groups become involved in the dissemination of information via meetings and/or newsletters.

The determination of local heritage groups has not only kept the conservation movement going, but even accomplished apparently impossible feats of renovation such as the Courthouse in Upper Woodstock N.B. (above) and the Langham Cultural Centre in Kaslo B.C. (below)

Demonstrations were once a frequent sight, but have declined in popularity.

(ii) Merchants' Groups

Merchants' groups are organized along lines similar to those of citizens' groups. They have been relatively more influential, and have scored some significant victories.

These groups are sometimes highly organized. On the other hand, many merchant groups are loose associations dedicated to "Self-Help" or to the "Norwich Plan", a highly successful scheme pioneered in England to promote voluntary and co-operative "Fix-up" campaigns in commercial areas. Organizations such as the Devonian Foundation and the Norwich Union Insurance Company have provided great assistance to the formation of such groups.

A more elaborate (and institutionalized) version of this approach is found in Ontario, where the *Municipal Act* foresees *"Business Improvement Areas"*. Such areas are created when two thirds of the merchants form an association, which can then *oblige* the municipality to form a *Board of Management* for the area. The Board budgets for improvement and promotion of the area; if the budget is approved by the municipality, funds are voted accordingly from municipal taxes raised within the area.

HERITAGE DAY

(i) Introduction

Anyone who believes that February is the shortest month in the year just because the calendar says so has never spent winter in Canada.

For some time, many Canadians (including, not surprisingly, a few labour leaders) have urged the proclamation of a national holiday in February. Many also suspect that this proclamation is strictly a matter of time, as soon as an upturn in the economy makes us imagine that we are a "Post-industrial Society" again.

Heritage Canada poster

Conservationists argue that if there is to be such a holiday, it should be dedicated to Canada's heritage. Canada is one of the few countries in the world with no such holiday. Heritage Canada and its member organizations undertook to hold celebrations on that day in February, even if no holiday has yet been declared.

Almost every promotional technique known to conservationists has been used on "heritage day", and consequently a review of heritage day activities gives a fairly accurate picture of the movement's techniques. Indeed, the promotion of heritage day and the development of promotional techniques has even been taken up by groups which are not conservation groups.

(ii) The General Direction of Promotional Efforts

The focussing of attention on heritage through Heritage Day is promoted by Heritage Canada and by local groups.

Some provinces, such as Alberta and Quebec, have dedicated different times of the year to heritage. That occasionally causes certain headaches for conservationists both in terms of co-ordination and also for the purchase of common posters, buttons, etc. In those provinces, some conservationists continue to stage events in February on the assumption that an extra day devoted to heritage can do no harm.

Heritage Canada is the primary co-ordinator of Heritage Day in three ways:
— through support for certain legislative initiatives
— through the media
— through its member organizations and friends

On the federal level, the Secretary of State promised a government bill to declare "Heritage Day" a statutory holiday in February, a measure which enjoyed support from all parties. . . . until grumbles were heard about the effect on productivity. Conservationists continue to hope that room will be found *somewhere* on the calendar for an appropriate holiday, but for the time being the notion of a statutory holiday in February is like the month itself: in the freezer.

That fact has not stopped Heritage Canada and other conservationists from making other overtures on behalf of "Heritage Day" even if it is not a national holiday. At Heritage Canada's request, the Governor-General and the Prime Minister issued statements supporting the ideals of Heritage Day; in 1976 seven provincial Premiers and twenty-two Mayors also declared their support for Heritage Day.

Press releases have been issued to ensure that the media are informed of all developments regarding Heritage Day at the national level.

Heritage Canada prepared a tabloid and an education kit for distribution to member organizations and others interested in the promotion of Heritage Day.

Local conservationists are urged to promote Heritage Day in the same way that Heritage Canada does:

— through support for legislative initiatives
— through the media
— through their own activities.

They are urged to write to the Prime Minister, the Provincial Premier, their federal Member of Parliament and Mayor expressing support for Heritage Day, and to ask other groups within the community to write as well. It is also suggested that their Member of Parliament and Mayor participate in the events organized to celebrate Heritage Day.

It is important that local media be kept informed of events in the community. Conservationists attempt to involve them in the celebrations on Heritage Day. There are many ways to do this:

— to contact the local newspaper reporters responsible for covering community events,
— to utilize public service announcements on radio or TV,
— to invite the local disc jockey to cover the events on Heritage Day,
— to arrange to have the local TV news show interview the organizers of Heritage Day activities.

From political hoopla to quilting bees, Heritage Day has generated activities from coast to coast

A list of suggested media contacts is forwarded by Heritage Canada to local groups.

It is suggested that conservationists pick events which are of interest to the community as a whole and to try to organize exhibitions and activities which will inform and involve people of the community in their *own* heritage; encourage other community and service groups to join with them in organizing activities and co-ordinate activities with theirs to ensure a more successful celebration; approach the schools in the community and suggest that they sponsor a debate, an essay contest, a heritage play or short story, and that the students be encouraged to dress in heritage costumes, demonstrate heritage crafts and skills, or participate in some other group activity on Heritage Day; settle on a number of events, appoint a Heritage Day co-ordinator to oversee their organization and start publicizing the Heritage Day celebrations at least two weeks in advance to try to orchestrate the media campaign so that it reaches its peak on Heritage Day.

Heritage Canada provides buttons and posters to each member organization to help promote Heritage Day. The buttons are stamped with Heritage Canada's symbol and the Heritage Day slogan: "Heritage has its day".

(iii) Case Study: Renfrew, Ontario.

Perhaps the most imaginative and active Heritage Day community in the country in 1976 was the little Ontario town of Renfrew (population 8,530). Its activities are a microcosm of all Canada. The following is a partial list of the town's activities.

The Mayor and Council proclaimed the day to be "Heritage Day" (without, however, making it a holiday) and gave assurances that they would assist the local conservation group, Heritage Renfrew, with its celebrations. The Council's proclamation was published in the town paper.

Heritage Day posters provided by Heritage Canada were distributed to the town's eight schools, public library, churches, and Main Street buildings. In addition, twenty-four Heritage Canada bronze pins were given to the schools as prizes for various activities. Sixty-five lapel buttons were sold at $1.00 each to raise money to defray program costs.

The day's organizers concentrated much of their attention upon schools. At one school, all students participated in a Craft Contest. Projects included: a bake sale using old recipes; a walking tour of old neighbourhoods; a display of artifacts of countries from which the area's pioneers had come; a collection of Indian and Inuit clothing; demonstrations of ice cream, butter and cheese making; and a history study of one of the area's early settlers. At another school, French heritage was stressed. Students participated in skating, square dancing and sleigh riding. Snow sculptures (of locomotives, horses, and cutters, and wishing wells) were produced. Many teachers and students dressed in nineteenth century costumes.

The Renfrew Collegiate Institute prepared a display called "How the Community Looks to Us": featuring about 50 drawings of early structures, the display was mounted for four days at the town's Recreation Centre. Another school produced one of the day's outstanding projects; an eight page tabloid on Renfrew history. The project was inserted as a special supplement to the town paper. One high school concentrated on a media-oriented piece: these students taped the reminiscences of senior citizens. The tape was broadcast on radio the evening of Heritage Day. Another school rented a local arena for a history day. Students and teachers dressed in pioneer costumes. The film "Old Renfrew", which had been made by the school's teachers, was screened. Over at still another school, halls and classes were decorated with student-made Heritage Day posters. A Heritage Canada film was shown and students listened to a round of special speakers. At one grade school, in addition to films and speakers, students enjoyed a variety concert. Outstanding efforts at the grade school included: "Herbie's

Heritage", a student-produced newspaper; a book of old songs collected by students; and an eye-catching poster display of "Heritage in Fashion".

On another front, the Renfrew Heritage Day organizers had great success enlisting the aid of local shops. They persuaded almost every shop to resurrect and display the items which might have been sold there long ago: for example; the shoe shop exhibited the "shoes of yesteryear"(!).

At the Renfrew Public Library, an open-house was held which featured paintings of heritage buildings. The library also displayed the local conservation group's survey of heritage buildings. Over at the Senior Citizens' Drop-in Centre the day was celebrated in several ways: Brownies and Guides entertained with a Community Sing; a Heritage Canada film was shown; and there was a display of nineteenth century farm implements. One church held an open-house, and hosted tours celebrating the building's 75th anniversary.

In the evening of the celebration period, 125 townsfolk attended the first annual Heritage Day dinner at a local motel. Old-time music was provided at the reception and a play written by the president of the local conservation society was performed. The play, set in 1854, told the story of early Renfrew settler Francis Hincks' plan to have the settlement develop industry.

The town's Kinsmen's Club joined Heritage Renfrew in promoting celebrations. The Kinsmen also distributed posters, advertised the dinner, and ran radio ads reminding Renfrewites of the day.

Almost all of these activities were promoted and co-ordinated by a *volunteer committee of ten local residents*.

PUBLIC PARTICIPATION — FORMAL TECHNIQUES

It may be argued that one of the first instruments of citizen participation is to appoint members of the general public to the Heritage Advisory Boards which are consulted by the ministers of most provinces. There are, however, other mechanisms which have a more pronounced grass-roots flavour.

The legal framework for public participation in land use controls varies according to the three forms of land use controls affecting heritage conservation in Canada.

The first form is environmental impact assessment, which is the land use control which regulates governmental projects; the second category includes provincial controls on designated heritage sites; and the third is general municipal land use legislation (bulk, height, design of buildings etc.)

The environmental assessment statutes mentioned earlier for Ontario and Alberta usually say that participation is in the form of a hearing which citizens can demand if they believe that the environmental assessment procedure is not being used properly. However, the ultimate mechanism available to American conservationists (the lawsuit) is not granted to Canadian counterparts under the Canadian version of environmental impact legislation.

The second category of controls includes provincial control on designated heritage property. In those cases, the cupboard is bare: there is no provision for public participation whatsoever, either to coax the government to designate a certain site, or in the supervision of alterations or demolition which are later conducted on the site.

The third category of controls is found in municipal land use planning. Rules respecting public participation at this level are scattered throughout provincial *Planning Acts, Municipal Acts*, city charters etc., and vary from place to place. The following, however, are some features which appear in the enabling legislation of most municipalities.

Since municipal governments have the greatest contact with land use planning, it follows that any private proposal to change the status quo must be submitted to the municipal administration. In most municipalities, such proposals are secret. Similarly, there is usually no provision stipulating that reports written on proposed plans for the municipality must be made public, or even that the terms of reference of those reports be published. As seen later on, those terms of reference can be crucial to the conclusions of the report.

Proposals for changes in the *status quo* are then submitted to the elected municipal council for its consideration. Again, there is usually no stipulation that either presentations to council or council's deliberations be made in public.

However, when the time comes for municipal councillors to vote on a proposed change, such vote must usually be made in public, and citizens must usually be given advance notice of the issue as well as the date of the council meeting. This meeting is the forum at which citizens can make their views known; however, there is seldom any statutory obligation for the municipality to give any details on the expected impact of proposed changes or alternatives thereto.

In one province (Quebec), citizens can force a municipal referendum on changes to municipal land use controls. In some other provinces, the decision of the municipal council can be appealed by the citizens to a provincially appointed board or to the provincial minister of municipal affairs. In the case of appeals to boards, there is usually a statutory obligation to hold a hearing; there is usually no such obligation in the case of an appeal to the minister.

In some places, citizen participation is ostensibly institutionalized in the form of citizens' advisory bodies; some have been mentioned earlier. Ontario's *Local Architectural Conservation Advisory Committees* (LACAC's) are expected to play a useful role in promoting conservation in that province. Many other cities across the country have set up similar committees.

Heritage Canada has been promoting the establishment of "foundations" which, to a certain extent, would institutionalize citizen participation in heritage areas.

These foundations would be directed by boards composed of representatives from governments active in renovating an area plus voting representatives of the heritage societies, citizens' groups, merchants associations and prominent agents in the community. The foundation would not only act as the liaison body for conservation activities, but would also receive government funds to carry on its own investments. Such foundations have been established in several cities.

The most elaborate schemes for citizen advisory committees are probably those of Le Breton Flats in Ottawa and the complex statutory system in Winnipeg. The latter has come under such vigorous criticism from the politicians that its future is uncertain: one commented "the best thing about these advisory committees is that they meet only once a month; the worst is that they meet once a month".

Whither goeth citizen participation? The catchword of a decade ago sometimes appears to be heading into the limbo of all ponderous clichés: partial institutionaliza-

The last five years have seen a variety of tactics to get the voice of conservation out of the cold streets and into warm city council chambers

tion followed by neglect on the ground of impracticability. Perhaps this is only the result of an economic downturn which has made some people impatient for government action unfettered by the time-consuming process of participation; if so, then we can hope that the momentum for participation will enjoy a resurgence when the economy does (if the economy does). But some people worry that the problem is deeper, i.e that the slowdown of participatory efforts is based on an inadequate number of citizens willing to participate.

Conservationists are generally more optimistic. Many believe that decreased attention is being paid to citizen participation because citizens' groups are now so common that they are no longer newsworthy. There is certainly supporting evidence in the heritage movement: new organizations are being established and joining Heritage Canada regularly. Conservationists recognize nonetheless that these are not easy times for citizen participation, and consequently they must work extra hard on the strategies which they will employ. Some of those strategies are described below, although the groups responsible would best go unnamed.

PUBLIC PARTICIPATION — SOME INFORMAL STRATEGIES

(i) The "Legal Beagle" Approach

One of Canada's more influential local groups has adopted a systematic policy of wooing lawyers into the organization. Its executive is now composed almost entirely of members of the legal profession. It has capitalized on its legal expertise by invoking the widest assortment of thoroughly obscure laws to impede unsympathetic development.

(ii) The "Mata Hari" Approach

Another influential local heritage group decided that co-operation with public officials could best be achieved as follows. Knowing that it enjoyed a good reputation as a respectable historical society, it systematically recruited wives of Cabinet ministers, and then set out to convert them into dedicated conservationists. Within short order, governmental decisions were exhibiting a far more sophisticated appreciation of heritage matters. No surprise there.

(iii) The "Bacterial" Approach

When Ontario enacted new heritage legislation in 1974, it empowered municipal councils to name "local architectural conservation advisory committees" or LACACs, a name which sounds appropriately similar to a certain kind of artillery.

Some conservationists expressed concern. The LACACs were given only an *advisory* function, and some people worried that many municipalities would establish them and then deem their own heritage duties discharged. In short, some conservationists feared that the establishment and operation of the LACACs would be used to *dupe* the public into a false sense of security.

More experienced conservationists gave a wry smile and said "wait and see".

As expected, a multitude of municipal councils had no objection to establishing LACACs, and used the opportunity to make lengthy speeches about heritage. They perhaps knew that there was little the LACACs could do to help protect Ontario's heritage against demolition. What they probably did not know was that the members of the LACACs would soon reach the same conclusion.

The LACACs had been given a mandate to study heritage ... which is precisely what they did. Many acquired considerable expertise. Furthermore, the nominees tended to be chosen among the community's more influential members. They did not take kindly to having their recommendations frustrated. The media have taken due note, thereby sensitizing public opinion.

In short order, and beyond the expectations of many politicians, LACACs have generated a political force to be reckoned with, and a powerful argument for more comprehensive legal action.

This, according to some people, is what some foresighted conservationists both inside and outside government had been expecting all the time. As one of them put it, "It's like a test tube. Give it the right ingredients, and you'll soon have conservationists swarming all over the place".

(iv) The "Woodwork" Approach

Some conservationists have decided to make themselves such a regular feature at municipal council meetings that they might be mistaken for part of the furniture . . . as long as the furniture speaks from time to time.

They claim that this approach not only leads to an unusual degree of intimacy with the council, but that over the long term it induces the council to equate conservationists with the public (or at least a significant part thereof). One distinguished conservationist became such a regular feature at council meetings that the councillors were reluctant to start meetings without her (!).

(v) The "Double-Barrelled" Approach

Citizens' groups are frequently divided over a persistant dilemma: is it better to maintain a low profile and attempt to make favorable deals with politicians in smoke filled back rooms, or should citizens' groups seek a high profile by loudly denouncing unfavorable projects? *The Old Boy Network versus The Squeaking Wheel*: it sounds like a horror story, and for many strategists it has been.

Conservationists in one major Canadian city believe that they have solved the problem: they have set up two organizations. One is composed of assorted plutocrats who regularly discuss conservation with officialdom between martinis; the other regularly foams at the mouth over alleged civic indifference toward conservation. The two groups exchange notes scrupulously. These conservationists hazard no guesses as to how long they can maintain this vaguely schizoid strategy ... but neither are they complaining about the results so far.

(vi) The "Pick-your-Victim" Approach

Although most jurisdictions have empowered their governments to protect endangered heritage, many officials have qualms about taking that giant first step in implementing the legislation. Many conservationists are convinced that the first designation of an historic site on private property is the most difficult: once the officials have swallowed hard and have designated private property, they will have less reluctance to protect endangered property in future over the cries of "creeping socialism".

Conservationists have often adopted the old engineering axiom that the shortest distance between two points is the path of least resistance: in some provinces, religious property was the first privately owned property to be designated for protection on the assumption that it would arouse the least controversy and opposition (a *sometimes* valid assumption). In some other communities, however, conservationists have sought, as the first building to be protected, a structure which was *bound* to arouse the owner's ire ... when that owner was already unpopular. For example, some conservationists out west have looked longingly at railway stations, knowing that few government moves are likely to garner as much public support as those that are *opposed* by railway companies (which rank slightly lower than gophers in popularity contests). On many a conservationist's bookshelf, Mazo de la Roche and Lucy Maude Montgomery are being joined by Niccolo Machiavelli and Saul Alinsky.

PART VI
HERITAGE IN ACTION: A CASE STUDY

CHAPTER 13

AN INTRODUCTION TO GASTOWN, VANCOUVER

HISTORICAL SUMMARY

On a drizzly September day in 1867, a former river pilot named John Deighton paddled into Burrard Inlet

Gastown, circa 1879

and unloaded two women, a dog . . . and a keg of whiskey.

He succeeded in attracting the enthusiasm of workers at a nearby sawmill(!), and within twenty-four hours his saloon stood proudly at what is now the corner of Water and Carrall Streets.

The City of Vancouver was born.

Deighton's taste for monologues earned him the notable title of "Gassy Jack", and the thirsty community that sprang to life around his august landmark became known as Gassy's Town or Gastown.

In 1868, Gassy Jack asked the government for a formal deed to the site on which he had settled. The request was refused. This was Gastown's first confrontation with bureaucracy. It was also the first occasion on which a government decision was disregarded.

No self-respecting metropolis, however, could long bear as unpretentious a name as Gastown; so when the new townsite was surveyed by the government in 1870, it was officially named Granville after the British Colonial Secretary.

The survey led to Gastown's second major problem with bureaucracy: the surveyors insisted on putting a street through Gassy Jack's saloon. This was Gastown's first confrontation with a highway system.

Eventually, an assortment of thirsty customers had to move Deighton's saloon. A century later, Gastown merchants would promise that Gastown would not be displaced again.

Maple Tree Square, 1886. This mean-looking crowd is standing at the door of Gassy Jack's old saloon

Law and Order: the entire Vancouver Police Department poses in front of City Hall, 1886

Shortly after British Columbia was led into Confederation by Premier Amor de Cosmos, the community petitioned for an increase in its one-man police force. Nevertheless, over ten years later William Van Horne would still warn visitors: "Keep your eyes open. These damned ... fellows will steal the pants off you". The bewildered Coroner noted that "so many bodies have been found, foul play is the only explanation". Despite Edmund Roper's assertion in 1891 that "a very much higher style of tone and thought prevails amongst the better classes on the Pacific Coast than in the rest of Canada", the local newspaper complained that "there is also too much of the old frontier 'don't give a tinker's d ... ' spirit on the Pacific Coast". This was not only reflected in the gambling and uncertain virtue of the community (a special place was permanently reserved for certain ladies at the Opera House), but in the community's level of intoxication. The newspaper had "general advice to the vicinity: dry up!"

By the mid-1880's, the Canadian Pacific Railway was planning to steam into the community, (and has been doing so ever since). Even though it was only a spur line, residents felt that it was time for Granville (or Gastown, as most people persisted in calling it) to take its rightful place among the cities of the world. Accordingly, the community was incorporated as "the City of Vancouver" that same month. It is allegedly the C.P.R.'s own William Van Horne who chose the name in honour of the 18th century captain who charted Burrard Inlet.

Elections were held. The Burrard Inlet area counted 175 names on the provincial voters' list, but the election was won by a tight margin of 242 to 225.

The election was won by the first of Vancouver's long line of mayors who were simultaneously involved in the real estate industry.

But it was a bad time for real estate: on June 13, 1886, the city went up in a cloud of smoke. The twenty-minute fire, according to the Mayor's desperate telegram to Sir John A. Macdonald, left 3,000 people homeless. The residents were undeterred: they promptly built the city over again, in what a Winnipeg newspaper called "the grandest display of indomitable Western Pluck the world ever saw".

This time, however, the residents took fewer chances: many buildings were built of masonry, lest the city pull another disappearing act. By 1892, the population had reached 15,000.

The peculiar economy of the area was reflected in its buildings. Since Vancouver was a "boom town", it sprouted an unusually high number of hotels. The growing role of Vancouver's port facilities resulted in a large number of warehouses.

The boom, however, was not continuous: 1892-98 saw hard times for North America generally, until Vancouver was infected with the gold fever of the Yukon in 1898.

Not all the money which was unleashed found its way into champagne-filled bathtubs: much of it was invested

The disintegration of an area, both physical and social

in buildings in Gastown. This euphorious construction boom spilled beyond Gastown's boundaries; indeed, by the time it ended in 1914, it had carried the business community all the way to Vancouver's present business district. Gastown was now being left alone . . . and thus began Gastown's fifty-year journey on the slippery slope of economic stagnation and social decline. The warehouses gradually emptied, and the hotels often became home for Vancouver's skid-roaders.

Gastown's future appeared to promise nothing but a few swigs of vanilla extract, and eventual obliteration. The resurgence which occurred instead is nothing short of an urban miracle; it is that miracle which is described in the following chapters. Gastown is now not only a protected and secure component of the living city, but it is even graced with the title of "historic site" bestowed upon it by the government of British Columbia in 1971.

Vancouver was launched like a ship: with bottles of booze (though certainly not champagne). This was done in the 1860's, and some people may wonder whether one can label such an area "historic".

On the other hand, Vancouver is one of the few major cities in the western world which can still display functioning buildings which represent the first twenty-five years of its existence.

The fact remains that Gastown represents the achievement of a society which, in many respects, was still a pioneer society. For that reason alone, it can rightfully be called historic. Its value is also environmental: it provides a needed alternative to the anonymity of the modern city. Its success in this respect is unquestionable, and can be measured in the area's continuing popularity among the residents of the city.

GENESIS OF THE CONSERVATION AREA

The significance of Gastown to conservationists in other communities rests largely in the method by which it was established. It was an uphill fight. Unlike most heritage areas in Europe, the notion of creating a

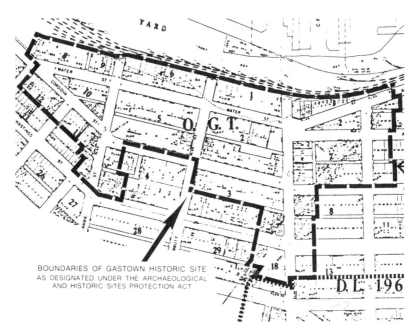

Re-emergence: the Gastown historic district and its location in relation to Vancouver's downtown

190

heritage area was not launched by inspired bureaucrats from the heights of a cultural affairs ministry: on the contrary, most government officials and planners intended to replace Gastown with highrises and freeways. They were dragged kicking and screaming into the Valhalla of conservation only by an aroused and militant citizenry. The account of that struggle is a worthwhile example to conservationists both in Canada and elsewhere.

Gastown as living history. The renovation of Maple Tree Square is opened by a lady who was born in the area at the very time that these buildings were erected

CHAPTER 14

THE BATTLE OF GASTOWN*

REVIEWING THE TROOPS

(i) Governments

Three levels of government were involved in the fate of Gastown.

The *federal* government was heavily involved . . . but *not* in plans to protect the area. It is extremely unlikely that the Department of Indian and Northern Affairs would, between 1958 and 1975, have attempted to designate any structures in the area as "National Historic Sites", let alone undertake efforts for their conservation. On the contrary, the federal National Harbours Board actively promoted (unsuccessfully) wide-scale destruction of the area through highway construction. Furthermore, federal funding was expected to help finance the destruction, to the extent of 18% of a multi-million dollar freeway project. This is many times what the federal government contributed to eventual

* The author gratefully acknowledges the help of the Vancouver Urban Research Group, whose book *Forever Deceiving You* was a valuable source of information for this chapter; some parts are reproduced by permission. The author also credits Gary Bannerman's *Gastown The 107 Years*, and Robert Collier's *Contemporary Cathedrals*. This chapter attempts to summarize the chronology of events as described by those texts; any errors or omissions are, however, the exclusive responsibility of this writer.

renovation of the area ($175,000 by 1974); but Gastown observers are optimistic that the federal government and its agencies will continue to support Gastown's objectives.

The *provincial* government was another participant. Its promotion of the area's destruction was not as noticeable as that of the National Harbours Board: it would have had to pay for a large part of the freeway complex. It was a provincial department (the Provincial Secretary) which ultimately had responsibility for *saving* Gastown from destruction in 1971. It has helped finance improvements to street facilities to the extent of $544,000 . . . again a fraction of the commitment it would have faced if Gastown had been destroyed by freeways.

Again, observers are hopeful that continued support will be forthcoming.

The *municipal* government of the City of Vancouver was the most ardent governmental proponent of the destruction of Gastown, until it finally reversed its stand and energetically promoted the protection of the area. The City's Planning Department was largely responsible both for the original plans for destruction and also for the current beautification programs. It has spent considerable sums on these programs, for which it has been handsomely rewarded: see Chapter 17.

Formal advisory bodies for the provincial and municipal governments are a very recent invention, and are described in Chapter 16. However, no survey of the participants, would be complete without mentioning the platoons of paid *consultants* (over $1,000,000 spent on transport studies between 1964 and 1969) whose reports did so much to help confuse the situation, as described later in this Chapter.

(ii) Associations

Several non-governmental groups had a decisive influence in protecting and promoting Gastown. A loose organization of proprietors decided to assemble in a more formalized group called the *Townsite Committee*.

During the 1960s, Vancouver's mayor expressed his views about the future of the city

A second organization was the *Community Arts Council*, an influential Vancouver cultural organization; its Civic Arts Committee was particularly active in organizing support for Gastown.

Further associations were set up by local merchants; three organizations preceded the current association, named the *Gastown Merchants Association*.

(iii) **Proprietors**

The main forces of the private sector on the demolition-redevelopment side were represented by the *"Project 200 Consortium"* which eventually was converted into a positive influence and a major contributor to Gastown.

The *media* were, for many years, intoxicated by the prospect of replacing Gastown with a sixty-storey disneyland; even after that prospect had disappeared, negative media campaigns continued to threaten the area, as described later. This attitude has now been favourably reversed.

An early meeting of Gastown merchants

(iv) The Merchants' Objectives

The decline of Gastown during the first half of the twentieth century had made it difficult to generate income from commercial properties. Many were held for speculative purposes.

There were, however, proprietors who hoped to use existing buildings for some reasonable purpose. They understood that it was pointless to renovate their own building if it were still surrounded by a decrepit environment: the only solution was collective action.

The owners therefore formed themselves into a loose association. The year was 1958. They successfully launched a clean-up campaign, which resulted in the repainting of many buildings and the renewal of public interest in the area.

It takes more than some paint and cleanliness, however, to guarantee the future of an area. It takes planning, legislation, financial support, and improvement of municipal services such as streets, sidewalks, lighting, etc. The owners consequently turned to the City of Vancouver for support.

There were problems in this approach. Few people considered the area particularly historic: most buildings were, after all, less than one hundred years old (the fact that they were very old by Vancouver standards was disregarded). Furthermore, few people considered the buildings aesthetically pleasing: the aesthetic *possibilities* of heritage areas were not clearly understood at that time.

In this sense, Gastown's case was highly similar to the situation currently prevailing in innumerable other Canadian municipalities.

There was a further problem. No community in Western Canada had ever attempted to create this kind of "heritage area" before. The entire concept was unfamiliar, and the financial prospects were totally unknown. Although there was some discussion of successful American precedents, the latter were very far away . . . and in any event, they were usually deemed inapplicable.

196

The association of proprietors did, however, have one major asset working for it: it was composed of *businessmen*. They were not architects, historians, planners, academics or "conservationists" (whatever those things were), and consequently could not be dismissed as lunatics by municipal politicians: most municipal politicians in Vancouver (and in Canada) are also businessmen.

They could thus count upon one of the peculiar paradoxes of Canadian municipal politics. A certain empathy often exists between commercial proprietors and municipal politicians because the latter are often commercial proprietors, or lawyers for such proprietors. A request for municipal action which is "good for business" frequently receives less critical scrutiny than a request to act "in the public interest". Furthermore, businessmen usually enjoy higher credibility in all matters pertaining to the projected prosperity of an area; this credibility is often essential.

Another reason for enthusiam was the creation of a much-heralded *Downtown Rehabilitation Advisory Board*. It was created by the civic administration, and in 1962 it went on a well-publicized trip to visit heritage areas on the American west coast (e.g. San Francisco's Jackson Square project).

At the same time, the Community Arts Council was launching showings of heritage films and slide shows. These presentations were used to proselytize municipal councils and chambers of commerce throughout the southwestern corner of the province. They had little effect elsewhere than in Victoria, but conservationists did not grasp the true density of political response at the time. Enthusiasm reigned supreme.

The proprietors formed a new group called the Townsite Association, and painting-up began in earnest. Their investment, they hoped, would prove to all concerned that Gastown had a viable future.

Consequently, despite all their problems, businessmen could approach the City in the early 1960's for support in Gastown with some guarded optimism.

The City, however, had other ideas.

OFFENSIVE MANOEUVRES ON THE WESTERN FRONT

(i) The Objective

Gastown was slated by the City for total obliteration: an even more powerful group of entrepreneurs proposed to bury the area under a gigantic complex of highrises, complete with freeway access. The complex was called Project 200. Pro-development newspapers had a field day.

An editorial writer of western Canada's largest newspaper wrote:

> In the area where Vancouver's first settlers had their homes and stores . . . where the first transcontinental train rolled in to be greeted by a cheering crowd of pioneers an exciting new redevelopment plan is under way. . . . The renewal area fronts on the harbor and replaces on a magnificent site structures decrepit and out-dated.

Project 200, as proposed atop the western part of Gastown

198

PROJECT 200

BOUNDARIES OF GASTOWN HISTORIC SITE
AS DESIGNATED UNDER THE ARCHAEOLOGICAL
AND HISTORIC SITES PROTECTION ACT

FREEWAY

Project 200 and its major access system

The one criticism which could never be levelled at this project was that of thinking small. It was to be the biggest commercial development ever proposed for Vancouver. Project 200 would:

— be composed of thirty-six buildings, ranging from 20 to 60 storeys high:
— need facilities for 120,000 people a day;
— spread over 8 blocks, many of which were in the heart of Gastown and which would be demolished;
— include office towers, apartments, hotel units, a department store and a covered shopping mall;
— require a transportation network that could include a northshore ferry and a waterfront freeway.

The business interests in Project 200 were powerful.

The initiator and main shareholder was Marathon Realty, the huge real estate arm of the even bigger Canadian Pacific Railway. Next came subsidiaries of Grosvenor-Laing Development, the international real estate giant based in England. Two large department stores also participated in the project.

199

(ii) Governmental Reinforcements

Major governmental support for Project 200 allegedly came from the Federal Government. According to the Urban Research Group, federal agencies had been working behind the scenes, mainly through the National Harbours Board and the Port Authority.

The Provincial Government backed the plan as well, but it had not pushed too hard for action ... perhaps because of the cost of access via freeway construction.

The strongest support probably came from City Hall. The ruling Non-Partisan Association (NPA) had held secure power for 30 years, and officials had made no secret of their co-operation with business interests. Certain city officials allegedly acted as private consultants to Project 200 developers; and with occasional exceptions, the NPA majority on council approved every Project 200 proposal presented to city officials.

Mayor Rathie supported the project. His son became a prominent executive in the project. Mayor Rathie's successor, Mayor Campbell, occasionally expressed support for renovation efforts but posed for publicity pictures while swinging from a wrecking ball. Mr. Campbell was himself a developer specialized in the construction of highrise buildings. First elected in 1966, he was re-elected in 1968 and in 1970 based upon his record of fostering "development".

(iii) Media Reinforcements

In the media, the notion of the planning process was still dominated by philosophical dinosaurs. As late as 1969, an editorial writer of the Vancouver *Sun* summarized his views in a book which gave a classic characterization of Utopia as a Canadian Los Angeles ... only more so:

> This would see whole areas of the work of building in the city's first two decades razed to make way for spectacular towers, plazas and shopping malls ... In the place of tired old buildings, too decrepit in many instances for their dingy, wood-floored upper storeys

to be rentable, soon would soar office, store and bank buildings, towering above underground shopping malls interconnected after the pattern of the new city center area of Montreal. Rainy Vancouver would find the underground "streets" of stores a boon in winter . . .

Excitingly, Vancouver was destroying without a qualm the things of its childhood to be better prepared for full stature in a fast-changing world. For the first time the suggestions of becoming a great and beautiful city implicit in some scattered office buildings and the complex of modern tall apartment buildings in the West End would begin to be reality . . .

There is a pattern of life evolving here which has not yet become apparent; a lively imagination can picture a possible future city which has become merely a machine-for-working, with its population's homes scattered far and wide over the south-western quarter of the Province . . .

The massive mountain range stands as it has stood for uncounted thousands of years; the inland sea grumbles as it has grumbled forever around its points, dashes over its reefs, roars through its narrows. But here, on the breast of the mountains and on the forehead of the sea, lies the jewelled city that men had built in a single human lifetime — Vancouver.

After statements such as those, a collective stampede by conservationists and planners was averted only by the intestinal immunity they had acquired: such statements had been heard frequently before in many parts of the country . . . and still are. In a growth-oriented consumer society, conservationists have become accustomed to the resemblance between the civic policy of many communities and the typical prospectus of a real estate development company.

(iv) The Manoeuvres Begin
1963

Massive commercial development in the area is suggested in several reports to City Council. Only one of the reports is requested by council; two of them are unsolicited from business interests.

(In Canada, one of the many ways that development interests get what they want from City Hall is by "loading the dice" with unsolicited reports. These are meant to stimulate the planning and engineering departments into making similar development recommendations).

According to the Urban Research Group, informal discussions with City officials take place concerning access to such a redevelopment (according to Project 200 spokesmen, negotiations begin in early 1975).

Fall 1964

Discussions concerning access to the development, now called Project 200, enter a more formal phase. Discussions and planning, both governmental and non-governmental, allegedly continue in secret.

October 1965

The Vancouver Sun *reports that land assembly is going on in Gastown.*

June 1966

Plans for Project 200 are formally unveiled. This is the first time the public officially learns of the proposal.

July 1966

City Council is convened to discuss a request made on June 28th by a Project 200 spokesman. He had called upon the City to provide planners, at taxpayers' expense, to help the developers with the project.

The City Council ponders its response in a meeting held behind closed doors.

Pursuant to the meeting, the City instructs its planners "to submit recommendations to council as to means of expediting approval of the project". At no time is there any question of examining the merits of the project itself.

August 2, 1966

The City chooses a firm from San Francisco to study access to Project 200. Unlike the study of access to Place Ville Marie (paid by the developers), this study is at taxpayers' expense.

The City commits $105,000 for the study (the City would eventually pay $212,000).

Meanwhile, a "Special Technical Committee" is established by the City to co-ordinate civic and private efforts in the project. It has five members, representing the National Harbours Board, provincial agencies, Canadian Pacific, the Project 200 consortium, the City Planning Department and the City Engineering Department.

The committee is given power to use all city employees that it needs for Project 200, at taxpayers' expense.

1967

Joint planning continues, but all documentation remains closed to the public.

Elsewhere, however, a major event is casting a long shadow over the project. As detailed later, access to Project 200 via a freeway encounters massive opposition. Unless access can be secured, the project will never be approved in its entirety. The developers henceforth request permission to build only one or two buildings at a time.

February 1968

Two years after the project is announced, Project 200 hires a firm of architectural and planning consultants from Massachusetts.

DEFENCE OF THE WESTERN FRONT

(i) Basic Strategy

The most vulnerable part of Project 200 was the access problem. Consequently, most of the opposition to it focussed on the highways plans, particularly those relating to the opposite end of Gastown. Those efforts are described later. Once that access became impossible, Project 200's offensive in Gastown petered out. This fact became increasingly evident after 1969.

Early renovation, Gastown-style

The crowd from Gassy Jack's saloon reincarnated on a renovation project

Interested citizens had, however, been using other techniques as well. The merchants had defiantly launched their own clean-up and *renovation campaigns,* despite the fact that elsewhere in Vancouver, buildings were being demolished even after renovation (e.g. on Robson Street).

Probably the most successful tactic, however, was organized by the Community Arts Council: it held massive *walking tours* of Gastown. On September 22, 1968, the first such tour encountered traditional Vancouver weather (rain), but nevertheless attracted over 700 participants. The proverbial writing was on the wall. Even Arthur Erickson, the architect working on the *freeway* proposals to provide access to Project 200, spoke on behalf of Gastown. The Mayor walked with the crowd, and pledged his "support for the efforts to restore Gastown.".

From that point onward, the Community Arts Council decided to organize more tours, and the political hazards of demolishing Gastown became increasingly evident.

(ii) The Offensive Slows Down
Summer 1968

In July 1968, the City's transportation Committee, chaired by the Mayor, submits its report to City Council. Although a short statement is issued to the press, the report itself is kept secret.

The following month, before any final word had been received concerning availability of access, the first building (albeit a small one) in Project 200 goes up in Gastown.

Sept. 22, 1968

The first walking tour of Gastown is a success.

January 3, 1969

The Community Arts Council formally requests clarification of Project 200 proposals from the City as well as assurances that basic planning principles will be observed. City Hall does not acknowledge the request.

Spring 1969

The developers face further problems. Some are internal; but some start coming from the City. Officials want the developers to pay a bigger share of the costs of a traffic bypass made necessary by the project. Two thirds of the land on which the road would be constructed is owned by the developers, one third owned by the city. One alderman suggests the companies therefore put up 2/3 of the costs, even though developers normally must pay all costs of roads made necessary by their developments. Wrangling ensues; however, the developers are not deterred.

On May 27, 1969, they announce that they will go ahead without a decision from the city over the bypass and without a development permit.

This gesture ruffles feathers at City Hall, and will have consequences soon afterward.

(iii) The Counterattack Intensifies
Spring, 1969

In response to public pressure, the City finally gives formal authorization to its planners to undertake a preliminary plan *for the revitalization of Gastown; officials had been encouraged by a popular revitalization scheme elsewhere in Vancouver.*

Furthermore, merchants open a "Flea Market" in Gastown. It attracts many shoppers, particularly since it is one of the few locations in Vancouver open on Sunday. Other merchants in Gastown also stay open on Sunday. This practice is entirely illegal, *being in violation of the* Lord's Day Act.

May 1, 1969

Gastown is extolled at a meeting of the Vancouver chapter of the Community Planning Association of Canada.

May 5, 1969

When two Gastown hotels are threatened with demolition, the Community Arts Council launches a petition *which gathers 550 signatures within a matter of hours. This is interpreted as a sign of public support for Gastown. Demolition permits are refused.*

June, 1969

A planning firm submits the first report on the conservation potential of Gastown. The report is very favourable, but the City "refers it for further study". The planners publicly accuse the City of procrastination.

July, 1969

The City's Planning Committee recommends beautification of Gastown.

Meanwhile, private recycling activity in Gastown intensifies.

An antique dealer founds the Gastown Gazette, and uses it to publicize the area.

(iv) The Offensive Encounters Logistical Problems
August, 1969

City Council refuses the development permit for another building in Project 200 until specific conditions can be agreed upon. The Vancouver Planning Director explains that letters of intent filed by the developers have not met requirements set by the City.

A developers' representative tells council that lawyers can settle everything "later". He says that a delay in granting the permit would "threaten the lifeblood" of

207

Project 200, (but that is apparently not serious enough to cause the developers to offer more for the bypass).

Accordingly, within one week council appoints a three man negotiating committee between the city and Project 200.

Two aldermen recommend that the city accept the promise of later co-operation regarding the bypass, i.e. grant a permit without a written agreement.

An opposition alderman makes a separate report calling for the developers to pay half the costs of the bypass. This proposal is labelled "sabotage" by other aldermen.

In the following week, City council gives the go-ahead for the project without a bypass agreement. It states, however, that the city will pay no more than 54 percent of the costs for the bypass. The Federal Government would be asked to pay for 18 percent of the bypass; if it agreed to this, Project 200 would have to pay slightly over one quarter of the cost, i.e taxes would pay for three quarters of the cost of roads around Project 200.

On August 26, an agreement is reached with developers over road costs. To this day, it is not known what the agreement was, since the meeting was secret and the record of proceedings is confidential.

(v) Final Volleys
November, 1969

In co-operation with the Community Arts Council, University of British Columbia Professor Setty Pendakur warns that Project 200 would have "serous economic consequences" for Vancouver. Without better planning, he says, the project could:
- *slow downtown traffic to a crawl*
- *cripple the port's efficiency*
- *displace up to 1,500 people*
- *attract thousands of residents to an area without adequate schools, parks, etc.*

Pendakur's findings are dismissed by Project 200 spokesmen.

In the opposite camp, a Vancouver Sun *editorial criticises some members of council for not giving sufficient co-operation to the project.*

Meanwhile, a festival entitled "Gastown Days" is launched by merchants with the help of a local church. It succeeds in attracting considerable publicity.

December, 1969

Part of the Project 200 contract is given to a company which is part of the corporate group responsible for the unsolicited 1963 report suggesting waterfront development. The same group was also responsible for the provincially-sponsored 1965 study that recommended a waterfront highway which, by coincidence, would provide access to Project 200.

The planning consultant who had repeatedly called for freeway construction, in transportation studies commissioned by the City, happened to be Vice-President of this company.

February 14, 1970

A group of Gastown merchants presents a "Valentine's Day gift" to the City: a statue of Gassy Jack Deighton standing on a keg of whiskey. Mayor Campbell promises to have it hauled away to the city dump, but the statue remains in Gastown.

Spring 1970

Work on another part of Project 200 begins in March 1970. Shortly afterward, Project 200 developers say that a hotel will be next. It is now obvious that they prefer to apply for civic approval for one building at a time.

The conservationists, however, have been cultivating links with some sympathetic planners in the civic administration, and increasing noises are being heard from within the administration itself for more serious study of the opportunities for conservation and renovation. Their efforts finally bear fruit in April 1970, when the City appoints a consortium of consulting firms to conduct studies for a "beautification project" in Gastown.

Meanwhile, the first large restaurant opens in Gastown. The Old Spaghetti Factory sets an example of structural recycling techniques: decoration is almost exclusively in movable items, and the building itself is reduced to its barest essentials. The restaurant soon averages 5000 customers per week, and leads to a chain of restaurants across Canada and as far as Australia. The manifest viability and popularity of recycling attracts increasing press coverage.

VICTORY ON THE WESTERN FRONT
Summer 1970

It has become obvious that Project 200 is less than a sure bet: it appears increasingly unlikely that an adequate

The Converted: Members of the old Project 200 consortium not only built harmonious infill projects such as Gaslight Square (left) but also renovated buildings and donated executives to Gastown activities.

solution would be found for access.

On the other hand, prospects for an effective (and popular) revitalization scheme appear better every day, particularly pursuant to the City's new planning studies. Gradually, more and more city officials are convinced that revitalization of Gastown is both more feasible and politically more expedient than flattening it; if Project 200 is to proceed, it can do so outside *Gastown's boundaries, or else in a scale and style compatible with the surroundings.*

Indeed, Project 200 developers start considering the possibility of constructing sympathetic buildings in Gastown on empty lots. This change in approach will ultimately lead to the construction of Gaslight Square *which is considered to blend well with its Gastown environment. Despite some financial difficulties with* Gaslight Square, *some developers become so supportive of Gastown that they lend top executives to Gastown community efforts.*

November 16, 1970

A major threat faces Gastown business. After several years of open violation of the Lord's Day Act, *the City Prosecutor finally threatens to a fine Gastown merchants who operate on Sundays.*

November 17, 1970

The merchants reply that they will collect the summonses in the centre of Water Street and burn them.

November 18, 1970

Upon the advice of conservationists, Mayor Campbell observes that if Gastown were a designated historic site, it might be possible to exempt the area from the Lord's Day Act.

December 2, 1970

An official delegation of three city councillors goes to the provincial capital requesting designation for Gastown and exemption from the Lord's Day Act.

February 2, 1971

Gastown is designated as an historic site by the province under the BRITISH COLUMBIA AR-

CHAEOLOGICAL AND HISTORIC SITES PROTEC-
TION ACT. Henceforth, no police action is taken against
merchants who are open on Sunday. It is not immediately
clear whether all politicians realize that the measure also
assures the protection of Gastown for the future.

THE OFFENSIVE ON THE EASTERN FRONT

(i) The Objective

Access to Project 200 was expected via an expressway.
There was some question where that freeway would go. It
was fairly obvious that part of it would follow the
waterfront; what few people knew was that it would turn
south, and obliterate a large part of the eastern end of
Gastown.

(ii) Offensive Manoeuvres
1959

*The original idea for a freeway through the area is
proposed in a report prepared over a three year period. The
report recommends forty-five miles (75 km.) of freeways in
and around the downtown, at a cost (in 1959 terms) of
some $500 million. The price tag apparently deters the city
from adopting the report, and consequently the public is
not informed whether the City has any proposed transportation plan.*

*If citizens had known of a transportation plan, they
could have debated its merits. Instead, various proposals
are made over the following decade to build parts of the
system; these proposals coincide with the 1959 plan, but
citizens have no idea what the City's long range objective
is.*

*Although the City has not approved the plan, it
nevertheless starts buying land in the proposed route.*
1961

*Council votes $115,000 for another study of the
highway system.*

*Its terms of reference are "to review, update and
recommend action on the 1959 plan and subsequent
proposals". Not surprisingly, its conclusions are basically*

the same as the 1959 report. (This result reflects a common strategy in the commissioning of some government reports: officials can virtually define the results they expect from their "expert" studies by defining the terms of reference.)

The Mayor then proposes construction of a short length of waterfront freeway . . . which leads almost nowhere. If the City accepts it, then future construction of the Gastown link will become inevitable in order to give the waterfront freeway somewhere to go; but the latter is not discussed.

No action is taken at the time. Instead, it appears that talks gradually begin concerning access to Project 200, which lays at the doorstep of the proposed waterfront freeway. That fact may or may not have been a coincidence.

1965

A study is commissioned on a viaduct project south of Gastown. Its terms of reference include a request for recommendations concerning the best way to link the viaduct with the waterfront freeway, i.e through Gastown. This is another "piece" in the overall plan.

The public still has no idea what that general plan is. In order to provide a credible clarification, the City commissions still another study. Again, the terms of reference specify that the consultants are to recommend a good route through *Gastown.*

June 1, 1967

After eight years, the plan is finally made public. Three consulting firms, including that of Canada's most publicized architect Arthur Erickson, propose a freeway which would carve through the heart of Gastown and neighbouring Chinatown. The proposal is accepted by Council almost immediately.

In public statements, the City emphasizes the freeway will be harmless because shops will be located underneath it. Erickson says the freeway is not really a freeway; it is "a building that happens to have roadway on top". Total cost is estimated between $350 million and $400 million.

June 10, 1967

A group of planners denounces the freeway.

June 13, 1967

Chinese businessmen denounce "the Great Wall of Chinatown". The Chinese Benevolent Association calls for a public meeting.

June 14, 1967

The Vancouver Chapter of the Community Planning Association of Canada denounces the freeway.

June 15, 1967

The City responds by halting further study of the Gastown-Chinatown route pending a public hearing. The project planner is asked whether the freeway could go elsewhere. In response to questioning, he answers, "that is beyond my terms of reference"over ten times, according to the Vancouver Sun. *It is suggested that perhaps the terms of reference should be broadened, and conservationists call for a new study. Seventeen briefs are submitted to the City by citizens' groups.*

June 17, 1967

The Vancouver Sun *reports: "City officials are reluctant to publicly discuss their opposition to (studying alternatives) but in private they say there is no need for a further study".*

July 17, 1967

The City has still not called for a new study. The Chinatown Property Owners Association denounces the City for "bad faith". The Chinese Benevolent Association states that the City is showing favoritism toward Project 200, constituting discrimination against the Chinese community. The Vancouver Visitors & Convention Bureau announces that it is "disappointed" with civic policy.

Late summer, 1967

The City agrees that further planning should take place regarding the route of the freeway. Critics are satisfied that other alternatives will avoid the Gastown-Chinatown route.

Instead, the City gives a final *announcement recon-*

firming the Gastown-Chinatown route; the date is October 17, 1967.

OCTOBER 17, 1967
This date is one of those extremely rare occasions in Canadian history when Canadians became sufficiently

indignant to carry their protest regarding governmental action into the streets. Mourning banners were draped from buildings. Residents and students marched in protest to the freeway proposal.

CITIZENRY MOBILIZES
October 18, 1967
Professor Hardwick of the University of British Columbia announces that the terms of reference of the planners were unjustifiably predicated on a Gastown-Chinatown route. Freeway opponents call for a public meeting.

The freeway planning officer replies that the freeway is

justifiable on the ground that it constitutes the most convenient access to Project 200.

October 23, 1967

Mayor Campbell says that the freeway will not be built for another ten to fifteen years anyway. Furthermore, it "will be an improvement rather than take away from Chinatown". He promises consultations, but opposes a public meeting.

October 24, 1967

The Vancouver Board of Trade denounces the "lack of consultation with the community".

October 30, 1967

The local Member of the Provincial Legislative denounces the planners' terms of reference. The lawyer for the Chinese Benevolent Association accuses the City of pandering to Project 200.

Mayor Campbell denounces opponents "playing politics with the Chinese community". He claims to have spoken to Chinese leaders who are "very happy with our decision". Another councillor describes critics as "a bunch of bovines out in left field chewing their cud, regurgitating and chewing again". However, they are narrowly outvoted in a City decision to call a public meeting.

November 1, 1967

Chinese businessmen deny Campbell's claim that they are "happy" with the decision.

November 5, 1967

Mayor Campbell denounces the calling of a public meeting as "a public disgrace and a tempest in a Chinese teapot".

November 7, 1967

The Executive Director of the Lower Mainland Regional Planning Board denounces the freeway.

November 8, 1967

Mayor Campbell states that it is too late to reconsider the freeway decision: "we are too far down the road".

November 10, 1967

The Vancouver chapter of the Architectural Institute of British Columbia denounces the freeway.

November 16, 1967

According to a City councillor, "the local voices raised in protest against progress on aesthetic grounds are unfounded".

November 17, 1967

The City engineer states that the freeway would redevelop an area that "needs rebuilding" anyway: "Most ladies wouldn't, nor do they, walk down Carrall Street at night".

November 23, 1967

Twenty-seven groups, even including the Vancouver Council of Churches, prepare briefs to be presented at the public meeting.

This in itself is an accomplishment, given the time in which citizens had to operate.

(It should be noted that in Canada, public hearings often come after a decision has been made — forcing the public into a position where it can only react to council's actions and recommendations in reports. In essence, the public is forced to try to assess, in a week or so, work which consultants have been paid to do with taxpayers' money over a period of several months or more).

The City council chamber overflows. One alderman claims that the public turnout is "fixed". The Vancouver Sun *describes the assembly as "riotous". The meeting is adjourned to a larger hall.*

December 7, 1967

Mayor Campbell states that the City was never really interested in the freeway anyway; all the City wanted was a viaduct south of Gastown and Chinatown.

December 10, 1967

A second public meeting is held. The Chairman of the Town Planning Commission reads the report supporting the Gastown-Chinatown route, and then dramatically resigns in opposition. Even architect Arthur Erickson expresses doubts about the freeway.

January 10, 1968

The City announces that it was never fully committed to a freeway: all it was really interested in was a viaduct south of Gastown and Chinatown. It approves the viaduct, and states that it is thereupon free to cancel the freeway proposal; it does so. No one knows where traffic from the viaduct will be fed to.

Spring, 1968

New plans are quietly undertaken for a freeway north of the viaduct, along the same route. The distinction is that the new freeway would be depressed, rather than elevated. Mayor Campbell would eventually announce that this proposal would not "have the same impact as spaghetti".

Summer 1968

In July, the City Council Transportation Committee is presented with a new waterfront distributor plan. Although the meeting is secret it is revealed that the proposal depends heavily on the co-operation of the National Harbours Board and the Canadian Pacific Railway, as well as financial involvement by the Federal and Provincial Governments. It is also disclosed that this proposal involves a connection to Project 200.

The federal National Harbours Board had launched its own freeway study. It had instructed its planners to obtain a final decision from City Council on the location of a freeway in the general vicinity of Gastown.

Council therefore commissions two more studies. The first is for another "piece" of the system; the second is for linkage to it. The latter study is conducted by a planner who is involved in Project 200 (see previous section). His report is presented behind closed doors. Council then instructs the other consultants to follow the planner's ideas.

Meanwhile, a provincially-sponsored study concludes that a rail network would provide better access to the downtown core. However, the City again commissions the same planner to do a "general" survey; his recommendation for transit is basically the same freeway system as advocated in 1959.

Public support for Gastown, however, is growing (as evidenced by successful walking tours), and political *realities are beginning to catch up with city officials; the studies are no longer taken sufficiently seriously to constitute a dramatic threat to Gastown.*

VICTORY ON THE EASTERN FRONT
1970

Any Gastown link in the freeway system, despite the report, is appearing increasingly hazardous. Another expensive part of the proposed network (a major bridge) is being considered simultaneously, and financial problems appear more pressing. Most important of all, however, is the question as to whether the whole effort is really worthwhile: is it worth the risk of massive public hostility to provide access to a complex which may never be built?

If Project 200 were smaller (i.e outside Gastown's boundaries), alternative access might be sufficient (e.g. the proposed bridge). It is still not entirely clear what the City's thinking is, but IT BECOMES EMINENTLY CLEAR THAT IT WILL NOT CONSTRUCT ANY FREEWAY THROUGH GASTOWN.

CHAPTER 15

LEGAL TECHNIQUES IN GASTOWN

LEGAL PROTECTION

(i) Statutory Authority

On February 2, 1971, Gastown was declared an historic site under the *British Columbia Archaeological and Historic Sites Protection Act.*.

This was a remarkable and audacious step for the provincial officials to take. There had been only rare instances of the Act being used to protect private property, and most of those were for strictly archaeological purposes. It had never been used to protect an area. The wording of the Act is both general and brief, even in the more refined version adopted in 1972:

2. (1) Where, in the opinion of the minister, land is of exceptional archaeological or historic significance, he may, by order, designate it as an archaeological site or as an historic site.

4. No person or agency shall knowingly (a) destroy, desecrate, deface, move, excavate, or alter in any way a designated site or remove from it an object.*

* This provision of the *Archaeological and Historic Sites Protection Act* was replaced in 1977 by a similarly-worded clause in the new *Heritage Conservation Act.*

(ii) Effects

As seen from the above wording, all alterations or demolition in Gastown are subject to provincial approval. The statute places no limits on the discretion which the government can exercise.

(iii) Procedure

The *Archaeological and Historic Sites Protection Act* did not outline either the procedure for protection nor that of applications for changes in the area.

Applications for changes are reviewed by the Gastown Historic Area Planning Committee (formerly the Heritage Area Advisory Board), described later. As applied to Gastown, the Committee functions in the following way. When a property owner makes an application for construction, signs, alterations, or change of use, the application is forwarded to the Vancouver City Planning Department. The application is then presented to the Committee for its consideration. If the Committee approves, the application then proceeds through the regular administrative channels until the permit is issued or refused. When the Board does not approve an application, the Committee attempts to reach a compromise with the owner, or it requests that the Director of Planning and Civic Development handle the matter on behalf of the Committee.

To date, only one demolition has been approved: the building was replaced by a parking garage of "Gastown-compatible" design approved by the Board. The building was applauded by many Canadian architects as the epitome of "harmonious" infill construction. Several new projects of harmonious design have been approved, most notably Project 200's Gaslight Square.

No. part of Gaslight Square [handwritten marginalia]

(iv) Authorities

The Minister responsible for the administration of the Act when it was applied to Gastown was the Provincial Secretary. Under the new *Heritage Conservation Act* (1977), that responsibility now belongs to the Minister of Recreation and Conservation.

Now Provincial Secretary [handwritten marginalia]

221

Since the terms of the Act were so vague, an advisory board was established: it is the Historic Sites Advisory Board.

Another primary function of the Board is to act as liaison for the various government departments responsible for heritage conservation. For example, the regulation of archaeological sites involves a number of departments, and problems of co-ordination have been noticeable.

Such problems have been felt in other provinces; but for some unexplained reason, they were particularly acute in British Columbia. For some time, the question of "who should be responsible for what" appeared incapable of being resolved to everyone's satisfaction, and even insiders had difficulty keeping track of the officials to whom duties had been transferred.

In view of this somewhat unstable situation, the provincial government wisely chose to rely heavily upon advice from the municipal level, to such an extent that provincial and municipal regulation of Gastown have become almost indistinguishable. This was not totally unforeseen, because the City government had finally promoted the establishment of the protected area, and had equipped itself with planners and advisors who were knowledgeable in matters relating to heritage conservation areas.

These developments were, however, somewhat surprising in the customary context of provincial-municipal relations; most government officials in Canada guard their prerogatives jealously, and do not let something as trivial as the inability to exercise them stand in the way of a good bureaucratic squabble.

Municipalities are frequently reluctant to permit provinces to assume direct jurisdiction over parts of their territory, and most provincial governments are equally reluctant to rely upon civic planners for their advice. In that perspective, the bureaucratic co-ordination shown in Gastown has been exemplary.

Indeed, it is not immediately clear whether this

arrangement is even totally legal; but to date it has not been challenged.

Pursuant to the "gentlemen's agreement" which evolved between the province and the city, Vancouver passed a by-law establishing the Historic Area Advisory Board. Since the terms of the Act were so vague, the Board was expected to recommend guidelines as to the kinds of structures to be protected, altered or demolished, as well as the style of infill construction. The Board would also make recommendations to the City concerning zoning and signage.

The Board's functions applied not only to Gastown, but also to Vancouver's Chinatown, which had been declared an "historic site" at the same time as Gastown. Separate boards were later established for the two areas.

The board (now called the Gastown Historic Area Planning Committee) has seven members plus a non-voting secretary representing the City Planning Department. The seven seats on the Committee are for development-oriented professionals (currently represented by the Architectural Institute of British Columbia), the University of British Columbia, the conservationists (currently represented by the Community Arts Council), the residents of Gastown, the Gastown Merchants Association, the Gastown Property Owners Association and the Townsite Committee.

The major function of the Committee has been to review applications for change in the area. The City's planner who is secretary of the Committee is heavily involved in giving design advice to prospective applicants in line with the policies outlined by the Committee. The Committee, like its predecessor, may also make recommendations dealing with other matters of interest to the heritage area.

The Gastown groups nevertheless felt that more was needed to assure proper liaison among all Gastown activities. They consequently begat a further organization, called the Gastown Historic Area Co-ordinating Committee; it is a registered society with a paid staff (currently of five people, including manager). The Gastown Festivals Committee first came under its wing, and then came projects such as the Marvellous Musical Clock (described later); now this committee is involved in a wide range of activities.

One of the most striking features of this set-up is that most ideas for the promotion of the area appear to flow from Gastown to City Hall rather than in the opposite direction. Naturally, this is a credit to the Gastown people who sit on these committees; but it is no less a credit to City Hall. The city's planning staff has exhibited superior co-ordinating talents which have had a catalytic effect and made this flow of ideas possible.

The City planning function for Gastown is carried on by the Central Area Division of the Department of City Planning in Vancouver. For further information concerning this planning function, contact:

> Central Area Division
> City Planning Department
> Vancouver City Hall
> 453 West 12th Ave.,
> Vancouver, British Columbia
> V5Y 1V4

Changes in Gastown tend to be organized or reviewed by the civic authorities on an *ad hoc* basis rather than in the perspective of a long-range development policy. This is because the City has no long-range official plan specifying in detail the proposed evolution of Gastown(!), although the area is mentioned for protection in general terms in the master plan of Vancouver as a whole.

(v) Compensation

There are no subsidies or fiscal advantages given to proprietors in the heritage area. On the contrary, property taxes have increased dramatically (in proportion to market values) as explained in Chapter 17.

The City rationalizes this policy in the following way. It claims that its investment in the area (street improvements, lighting, etc.) represents an indirect subsidy

224

insofar as it increases market values.

(vi) Integration into Development Policy

British Columbia has no environmental assessment act, which would compel the province to file reports if it threatened a part of the heritage area. However, it appears that the province is bound by the designation of Gastown as an "Historic site", and consequently must consult the Minister of Recreation and Conservation when it proposes to take action in the area. This obligation may be difficult to enforce because of the "locus standi" problem mentioned earlier. It is not immediately clear to what extent the province has effectively integrated protection of the heritage area into its development policy.

The City is also bound by the designation of the area as an "Historic Site". To disregard the designation would undoubtedly be an offence. As with provincial infractions, it is a moot point whether any citizen would have standing to take the city to court; his chances of success however, might be reasonable. Consequently, it is in the City's interest to integrate protection of the area into its development policy.

SUPPLEMENTARY MEASURES

Several municipal by-laws were passed subsequent to the designation of the area under the *Archaeological and Historic Sites Protection Act.* These by-laws regulated details of the heritage area.

The two most important by-laws involved new controls on uses and signs. Incompatible uses were discouraged, compatible uses were promoted in an area which had not previously foreseen them, and highly comprehensive sign guidelines have been promulgated.

SELECTED PROBLEMS

(i) Maintenance

The city's power to regulate maintenance is expressed primarily in the "Tidy Lots By-law". There has been no

225

apparent attempt to use this power to compel the maintenance of buildings in Gastown which remain unrepaired.

(ii) Radius

Nothing protects Gastown from unsympathetic construction immediately beyond its boundaries. An enormous and totally unsympathetic building, built by the public authorities, is now located within a block of the area.

(iii) Building Codes

In order to recycle a building, there is a legal prerequisite that the building be brought up to building code standards.

Until recently, some proprietors were able to deal with this problem more effectively than others. Entrepreneurs such as Larry Killam developed considerable skill in solving building code problems; others were less fortunate. It took some three and half years of negotiation before the City would issue a permit to recycle the Mussenden Building, a five storey brick building of post and beam construction which had been partially destroyed by fire.

Some entrepreneurs felt the City was being too reluctant to recognize equivalents for building code specifications. This debate, however, has allegedly become academic. Under recent amendments to the building code, recycled structures must now be capable of withstanding an earthquake equivalent to 7.2 on the Richter Scale ... although the major seismic threat to Vancouver allegedly comes from tidal waves, not earthquakes.

This new requirement of "seismicproofing" has aroused considerable consternation among Gastown proprietors and conservationists. They argue that it is a disincentive to recycling and as such will ultimately lead to deterioration rather than strengthening of buildings in the area. One conservationist commented: "Gastown's future is interesting but doomed". Although most interested parties would disagree with this bleak appraisal, there is agreement that the building codes should pay more attention to the special needs of recycling activity. The city has launched high-level studies in search of solutions to this problem.

(iv) Enforcement

Although the governmental advisory bodies in Gastown have pointed to some outright violations of protective legislation, it has occasionally taken years to obtain remedial action. Violations of signage regulations are a case in point. As mentioned earlier, there is little that citizens can do to correct this situation short of legislative reform.

(v) Government Action

As mentioned earlier, the enforceability of Gastown planning priorities vis-a-vis government agencies is weak.

Federal agencies such as the National Harbours Board are free to disregard Gastown's objectives. Accord-

The owner responsible for this illegal demolition in the Chinatown historic district next to Gastown paid a fine of $10.00

ing to some local representatives, it is only recently that arguments for greater co-operation have finally prevailed; observers do not know what the government has up its sleeve, but they are at least optimistic.

Provincial agencies allegedly fare little better. Although the area now enjoys good relations with agencies such as B.C. Hydro, merchants claim that co-operation was obtained only after unduly strenuous effort. Observers hope that this problem is now a thing of the past.

(vi) Access to Information

Much government information affecting the future of Gastown remains secret.

For example, the National Harbours Board was asked in 1972 what it would do with the waterfront which faced Gastown and which it was busily filling with landfill. N.H.B. Chairman (and ex-mayor) Rathie replied: "I shall have to take the position that there is no need to discuss this further". It is still not clear what the N.H.B. is planning to do with its property, although there is currently more optimism for co-operation than before.

This optimism is based upon two factors. The first is that the N.H.B has permitted a market to be set up on its property: this suggests that "its heart is now in the right place." Second, the N.H.B. recently astounded all observers by actually asking for people's advice concerning the future of its property. Despite the secrecy involved, conservationists have the consolation of knowing that the government appears benevolent.

CHAPTER 16

PROMOTION

"A businessman in Gastown shouldn't think like a proprietor; he must think like a promoter."

Larry Killam

"To communicate is the beginning of understanding."

Gastown Handbill

THE PROBLEM

The previous chapters have recounted, in passing, some of the promotional techniques used in the early days of the Gastown revival. The walking tours, the local newspaper, Gassy Jack's statue, etc. all had a favourable effect upon the public's perception of the area. However, many problems remained.

During the late 1960's, the hippie movement "adopted" Gastown, which became a kind of Haight-Ashbury of the North. That meant that Gastown soon developed an assortment of positive and negative factors corresponding to the features of the movement itself.

On the positive side was an enormous resurgence of handicrafts. This development was a logical extension of hippiedom's disillusionment with industrial society and its desire to return to simpler livelihoods. Hundreds of people became involved in the production and sale of handicraft goods on a highly informal basis. One witness recalls: "For $100, I remember buying an entire 'business', complete with shop, inventory and dog".

Predictably, these people professed no interest in bureaucratic niceties: it is estimated that only 18% of merchants held the obligatory business licence. This entire phenomenon gave Gastown an unusual air of spontaneity, and encouraged those who worried about the gradual disappearance of Canadian handicrafts.

As usual, however, it was hippiedom's weakest point which was exploited by the press: its propinquity to the drug cult.

For reasons which are still unclear, the media chose not to attack drug abuse *per se,* but rather to blame the entire phenomenon on Gastown itself. One local broadcaster urged everyone to stay out of the area. Even foreign newspapers got into the act:

> *"Cheap pubs and sleazy places have been turned into dens for drug addicts in which young people are abundant. The streets there, especially at night, are horror scenes. This is the result of being a close neighbour to the United States where drug addiction is a national tragedy."*
>
> *Pravda*

Mayor Campbell joined the chorus. This is probably the only occasion on which Mayor Campbell and *Pravda* agreed on anything . . . which in itself is ground for suspicion. Mayor Campbell, however, would not be outdone in his choice of words. He announced: "There's a horde of dirty hippies invading Gastown with syphilis in their packsacks."

That statement was, of course, unfair. Although Gastown had a large concentration of hippies, it was by no means exclusively a hippie haven: for example, it also had one of Vancouver's highest concentration of law offices and advertizing agencies. It was equally unfair to accuse the entire hippie community, without exception, of being "acid freaks". The rhetoric continued nonetheless, and the stage was being set for confrontation.

RIOT
July, 1971

An open-line broadcaster begins day-today attacks upon Gastown as an unsafe area. Mayor Campbell joins in the denunciation implying, as one broadcaster put it,

230

"that one would be risking his life by entering any Gastown business establishment."

By the end of the month, several meetings have been held by the Gastown Merchants Association to deal with the situation. The possibility of suing the Mayor is hotly debated but turned down. The Mayor is requested to be less sweeping in his denunciations.

August 7, 1971

A group of hippies, in alleged response to the Mayor's "provocation", decide to stage a "smoke-in". It would be a demonstration in which a "giant marijuana joint" (made of straw) would be burned to symbolize defiance of civic statements.

Several hundred participants and spectators arrive. Unknown to them, back alleys are already filled with mounted policemen decked in full riot gear; alleys also contain vans with more policemen inside. The evening is very hot and humid. The policemen have no water or washroom facilities, but must wait there for almost two hours before being ordered onto the streets.

August 7, 1971

Some hippies leave the main group and climb the walls of a nearby building. Others slap a bus rolling by. A high-ranking police officer appears with a megaphone and orders the crowd to disperse.

He does not realize that his megaphone is out of order.

The crowd does not hear him. Since the crowd does not disperse, the police are finally ordered into action. The mounted riot squad charges the crowd and pandemonium breaks loose. In the words of one broadcaster, "it was a miracle that no one had been killed".

Two aldermen are witnesses. Their testimony ultimately leads to a formal inquest which reprimands police behaviour. The harm, however, is done: unless immediate remedial action is taken, Gastown is scheduled to become the site of more bloody confrontations and the area is doomed.

August 8, 1971

Larry Killam tries unsuccessfully to bail out the scores of young people who had been hauled off to jail the night before. Radicals in the streets start organizing for a major confrontation with police scheduled for the following Saturday. Critics of the police claim that these "radicals" are agents provocateurs hired by police to rationalize the recent purchase of expensive riot gear.

The Gastown Merchants Association holds emergency meetings which will continue all week.

August 9, 1971

The Gastown Merchants Association hatches a plan to pre-empt confrontation and promote reconciliation at the same time. It proposes a gigantic "patch-up party" or "peace party" for the following Saturday, to which it invites civic officials, policemen, their wives, and the hippies. City Hall gives approval, but the Mayor refuses to attend; he is the only member of City Council to do so.

August 14, 1971

The peace party is an unprecedented success. 25,000 people jam the streets of Gastown. "Police constables chatted cheerfully with the same hippies they were chasing one week earlier." Costs are paid by local merchants. The City had been asked to pay for 1000 chrysanthemums, but the Mayor refuses.

As hoped for, the event succeeds in reconciling officials, policemen, and Gastown people: it is a turning point in public co-operation. It also sets an example for future events, on which the businessmen promptly follow up.

PROMOTIONAL STRATEGY

The riot and its aftermath had taught an important lesson: it would take more than the fine words of the *Archaeological and Historic Sites Protection Act* to assure Gastown's future. *Public support* was of the first importance, and hence promotion would become a major and continuous preoccupation. As one merchant said in 1972, "the only thing Gastown has to fear now is apathy".

Accordingly,the merchants devoted considerable time to the staging of events which would capture media attention and the public imagination.

The basic strategy, of course, was no different from that adopted by the Roman emperors: they offered the public "bread and circuses". Since this is probably the oldest "gimmick" in the books, they had to adopt some new twists.

"THE WAY TO A MAN'S HEART . . . "

The "bread" part of the strategy was taken on in straightforward fashion by a nearby department store. Periodically, it would invite the population of Vancouver to enjoy a low-cost breakfast. This event became assimilated to the festivals called "Gastown Days". The event attracted media attention, particularly in view of the site: breakfast was being served in the store's *garage*. As usual, something which would appear nonsensical elsewhere invariably would attract public support in Gastown.

A more ambitious plan was the creation of a farmers' market in Gastown. The market idea faced one minor problem: it was entirely *illegal,* thanks to British Columbia's maze of marketing board statutes.

Gastown merchants, however, had not been deterred

by bureaucracy before, and they were not about to start.

A "convoy" was organized among sympathetic farmers in the British Columbia interior. The "convoy" was "escorted" by guards armed with brooms. Under the carefully orchestrated glare of media publicity, and while resisting arrest by the Royal Canadian Mounted Police, it left the Okanagan Valley for Vancouver.

It was led by the nephew of World War II Field Marshall Erwin Rommel.

Many organizers were arrested, but they made their point. Public opinion detered the provincial government from imprisoning the organizers; instead, the laws were changed to permit the market, and it became a regular and popular feature in Gastown.

THE FESTIVALS

(i) General

Gastown merchants soon realized that co-operation with city officials was indispensable for the efficient organization of festivals. Consequently, they made a point of inviting civic representatives to sit on various organizing committees (now consolidated in the "festival committee"). This arrangement worked well, since the civic representatives tended to be planners who were already sympathetic to the aims of Gastown. These representatives soon found themselves performing an important liaison function in assuring that such things as street closings and police co-operation were obtained.

There are now six festivals affecting Gastown.

(ii) St. Patrick's Day

In the early 1970's, the owners of several Irish pubs in Gastown concluded that Vancouver needed a St. Patrick's Day Parade. By coincidence, the parade would terminate in Gastown, within easy distance of their pubs.

As with all festival events, this event is now planned by a committee (the festival committee) responsible to the Gastown Historic Area Co-ordinating Committee which is a partnership of local groups operating with assistance from the City Planning Department.

234

Participants in the Gastown Rain Festival searching vainly for some showers.

(iii) The Rain Festival

Vancouver is not really Vancouver without rain. Rain is a part of the City's heritage. It was therefore only appropriate that Gastown should hold a festival in honor of the ubiquitous drizzle . . . although the feature presentation of this April festival (a rainstorm) has occasionally been "sunned out".

The launching of the landlubbers' Bathtub Race

The major event in the festival is the Landlubbers' Bathtub Race, in which bathtubs speed through the heart of Gastown.

Another event is the Rainbeaux Arts Ball, which raises money for the festival committee.

(iv) The Heritage Festival

June is heritage month in Vancouver, and many events are staged in Gastown, as well as in the rest of the city.

Gastown is an important location for many of the "folkfest" activities. There is a parade, and on some days the streets are closed for street dancing, music, and a beer garden.

Gastown planners join the festivities in preparation for the Bicycle Races

(v) The Bicycle Races

In August 1972, the Gastown Merchants Association organized bicycle races through Gastown. The event continues to be held (despite the cobbled streets) and attracts substantial crowds. The main "Grand Prix" is preceded by children's races and by an assortment of strange events such as costume races. Beer and wine are sold in the street, and some profits go to the festival committee.

(vi) Gastown Days

Subsequent to the famous 1971 "peace party", the most outstanding success in promotional terms for Gastown has been the two-day festival entitled "Gastown Days".

The festival began in 1975 when the Merchants Association succeeded in obtaining civic permission for some temporary street closings. The merchants further obtained a provincial licence to sell beer; the "premises" in which they would sell it were listed as the streets themselves. At the time, British Columbia had undergone a two-month beer and liquor strike, and Vancouverites were getting very thirsty. In a series of brilliant legal manoeuvres, the Gastown Merchants Association succeeded in *compelling* the issue of over 500 cases of beer to itself. It relayed the brew to the local pubs

237

(who set up sidewalk and street outlets), and Gastown succeeded in attracting between 250,000 and 300,000 people during the two-day festival.

The festival now includes a wide variety of events during the last weekend in September. Some thirty or forty ethnic dance and music groups perform on two stages set up in the streets. Street theatre is also performed. These various groups perform until evening, when dance bands take over and the streets become giant dance halls.

One of the most popular events at the festival was a casino. As with so many great Gastown successes, it was quite illegal. It had been sanctioned as a "lottery", and officials chose to think of it as a lottery which just happened to include roulette wheels and blackjack tables.

When the festival ended and profits were counted, provincial officials saw the wisdom of changing the law. The casino was legalized . . . but under so many restrictive conditions that in 1977, the meagre profit margin made the utility of the whole exercise questionable. Some organizers wonder how much happier they would all be if the province had not bestowed the blessing of legality upon them.

The citizenry appears happy enough: the average attendance at the festival over the weekend is now estimated at slightly over 200,000 people.

(vii) The Christmas Festival

During December, Gastown merchants are encouraged to decorate their premises with elaborate Christmas decorations. Carollers are invited to Gastown to sing, and hot coffee is served in the streets.

(viii) Results

The festivals have a number of results.

From the merchants' standpoint, they are useful because they are profitable. Not only do they attract people to Gastown (who then browse in the stores), but they are even profitable in their own right: the various

The statue of Gassy Jack surveys the festival crowds in his town

beer licensing and sales transactions usually give rise to a profit of $3000 to $4000 per festival (except for Christmas and St. Patrick's Day) for the organizers.

From the conservationists' standpoint, there is some division of opinion. The purists argue that the festivals have a mercenary character and are, on occasion, less than totally dignified. The merchants reply that such characteristics correspond perfectly to the original character of Gastown.

It appears that the majority of conservationists must agree with the merchants on this point, and also agree that the festivals are working effectively to bring people into Gastown and to popularize the area. These objectives are commendable in themselves, and also provide the economic base which underlies continuing recycling activity.

MISCELLANEOUS TECHNIQUES

(i) Costumes

At first, numerous merchants would launch promotional campaigns with barkers or other employees dressed in outlandish costumes. This technique soon lost its novelty, and now costumes tend to be worn only during festivals.

(ii) Resident Curiosities

The merchants who promoted Gastown's revival during the late 1960's encountered an unexpected obstacle: Ace Aasen, the most cultured and articulate of the Skid Road residents questioned how the conservationists could undertake such works without *his* permission. He had, after all, appointed himself "Mayor of Gastown" . . . a title which no one, in the Skid Road days, had chosen to contest.

As usual, the merchants saw publicity potential. They provided him with appropriate top hat, tails and cane, and gave him the best room in the Hotel Europe. In return, Ace became a kind of "goodwill ambassador" for the community, and is locally recognized as "His Worship

The Gastown Steam-Operated Marvellous Musical Clock, financed by profits from the Gastown festivals

the Lord Mayor of Gastown".

This set off a flurry of other "appointments". Gastown soon had a "Governor", a "Grand Admiral", and even a self-appointed "Papal Nuncio". After initial publicity, the media became bored ... except with "the Mayor", who continues to enjoy publicity.

(iii) Contraptions

As mentioned earlier, Gastown entrepreneurs donated the statue of Gassy Jack to the City, and received worthwhile publicity for their efforts. The City is expected to take care of maintenance, although the City failed to do so when the statute was first damaged in 1969.

Gastown groups have now presented the city with an encore. It is the world's only steam-operated musical clock. Its appearance is sufficiently ostentatious and nonsensical for merchants to believe that Gassy Jack would have approved.

(iv) Tours

By the early 1970's, when the battle of Gastown appeared won, there was a reduction in interest by conservationist groups in organizing walking tours. There was an increasing interest among students, however, in the Gastown phenomenon. There were no governmental initiatives to provide educational tours; consequently, some conservationists established a company named Vancouver Historic Insights Limited to conduct walking tours and show films of the area.

The company, within a few short years, guided some 130,000 students through the area.

This company rendered a public service, and hoped to receive government backing: it could not hire guides, show films and rent premises on a break-even basis otherwise. For nine months, it received provincial subsidies; subsequently, all government funding was refused. The company struggled on in the red for almost two more years, until it finally had to discontinue this service.

CHAPTER 17

ECONOMIC ASPECTS*

INTRODUCTION

When attempting to measure the success of Gastown, the observer keeps stumbling over great masses of economic statistics. This strikes the purist as unromantic, even crass! Are there no Byrons and Shelleys to sing praises of Gastown's aesthetics? Are there no Charlotte Whittons to declaim on its social consequences?

Indeed there are: newspaper articles, tourist brochures and miscellaneous endorsements are supplying an abundance of purple prose from every direction.

Some of that prose is more significant than most. For example, Inspector MacLeod of the Vancouver City Police stated:

> Most important from my perspective is the ability of the Merchants Association, Police and other service agencies to work together with a minimum of red tape and bureaucratic hassle. The result is a viable, lively area quite easy to police, one we can be legitimately proud of."

Most evaluations of Gastown's aesthetic and social success are nevertheless subjective: these factors are

* The author gratefully acknowledges the generous assistance of the Vancouver City Planning Department, whose *Gastown Economic Study* and *Gastown's Visitors' Survey* form the basis for parts of this chapter and which are reproduced (in part) by permission.

243

Gastown by night. Police assert that safety has been significantly improved since renovation began

almost impossible to quantify. If one wishes to *prove* the success of Gastown in *mathematical* terms, one is stuck with the ubiquitous economic findings. Consequently, the quantitative appraisal of Gastown's performance will discuss that loathsome subject, money.

INVESTMENT FROM THE PUBLIC SECTOR

(i) Purchase, Renovation, Subsidies

The extraordinary feature demonstrated by Gastown is the enormous distance which can be covered by a relatively limited public investment.

There is, unquestionably, a long distance to go: Gastown still has a large percentage of under-utilized space which will probably remain that way until further economic or fiscal incentives are made available. Such has also been the experience of other protected areas such as Old Montreal. Nevertheless, Gastown provides an example of the impetus which is created simply by street improvements and a co-operative association of proprietors and merchants.

For all intents and purposes, Gastown has not seen *any* level of government

a) buy buildings;
b) restore buildings itself, or
c) subsidize renovations.　　　✓　　　*CMHC - Stanley + oF*

This pattern has, however, had some negative characteristics. Since much of the responsibility for Gastown's revival was cast upon the merchants' shoulders, their costs had to be amortized through increased rents. The days have long gone when, for $100, one could take over "a business, complete with shop, inventory and dog".

This has had a severe dislocating effect upon the handicrafts which were once identified with Gastown. Although it is true that the handicrafts were dealt a severe blow by the demise of the hippie movement, at least a partial presence could have been maintained if there had not been a dramatic price increase for commercial space. It is now almost impossible to detect in Gastown any traces of the bazaar atmosphere which was once a major attraction.

There are increasing calls by conservationists for some level of government to buy some commercial space and to make it available to the handicraft producers at a cost proportionate to 1970 levels.

Similarly, conservationists are asking why government offices still have a negligeable presence in Gastown. Most government offices in Vancouver are leasing downtown office space (at taxpayers' expense) at approximately twice the cost of top-quality recycled space in Gastown. The area, which is deemed optimal by some 100 lawyers and six of Vancouver's nine advertizing agencies, still appears beneath the dignity of the bureaucrats. If levels of government were to decide to save taxpayers' money by locating some offices in Gastown, it appears that further revival would be stimulated.

(ii) Compensating Social Hardship
Some 400 low-quality (but low cost) housing units have been lost in Gastown. The pressure for a governmen-

tal commitment to compensate social hardship has been virtually non-existent . . . possibly because the Skid Road "residents" attracted relatively little sympathy.

This attitude has been unfair. Although it is true that some of the Skid Road residents were alcoholics, the proportion is reputedly no greater than in society as a whole. Indeed, the equation between a Gastown residence and alcoholism was absurd: many residents could not even afford alcohol. Most "Skid Roaders" were pensioners who had retired on unindexed pensions and who could not afford to live elsewhere than in Gastown's cheap hotels. The little money that they had was often stolen by thugs who preyed on Gastown's defenceless. In the words of one planner, "they had committed the worst crimes of our society: namely, they were old and poor. In many cases, they were prisoners of their rooms."

They were, however, an embarassment: they upset those who came to Gastown for pure escapism. Until recently, few people could detect any government action to deal with this problem.

The private sector has, however, made considerable efforts on its own. For example, the owners of the Hotel Europe pay such scrupulous attention to the economic affairs of their down and out clientèle as to constitute a "social service" in the eyes of one broadcaster. Elsewhere in Gastown, conservationists purchased two buildings with the intent of providing accomodation for the "winos". They hoped that commercial rental from the ground floor would subsidize rents on the upper floors. Although they obtained low-interest C.M.H.C. funding, this private project has been "less than successful".

Another form of displacement has been that of handicraft workers, mentioned earlier.

In both of these cases, conservationists wondered when, if ever, governments would undertake comprehensive action. The City has at least taken some worthy preliminary steps by entering into agreements with several hotels to provide the old residents with inexpensive decent accomodation. Conservationists hope that

246

this sign of good intentions is also a sign of things to come.

(iii) Care of Surroundings

Almost all public investment took the form of street improvements.

Between 1970 and 1975, the City invested $1,800,000 in capital improvements in the area by acquiring land, undergrounding utilities, and improving the appearance of Maple Tree Square, Blood Alley Square and Water Street.

Total investment in these three areas by the Federal Government amounted to $175,000 and investment by the Provincial Government to $544,000.

The utility companies spent $459,000 and property owners spent $926,000. Altogether, $3,175,000 has been spent on these three beautification schemes between 1966 and 1974.

PRIVATE INVESTMENT

(i) Introduction

Two major influences provoked considerable private investment in the area.

First, the civic improvements obviously made the area more desirable, particularly for retail purposes.

Second, the designation under the *Archaeological and Historic Sites Protection Act* as well as the City's commitment to the area gave property owners and merchants additional confidence in the future of the area, thus freeing some loan capital for renovation efforts.

(ii) Scope of Investment

From 1965 to 1973, the value of building permits issued increased by 2,180 per cent from $42,000 in 1965 to $971,000 in 1973. If the period between 1965 and 1974 is considered, then the value increase amounted to an estimated 3,300 per cent. This compared with a City-wide increase of 59 per cent for the same period. The value of the building permits for the total period 1965 to

The illustrations on this and following pages demonstrate the achievement of the private sector

1977 amounted to approximately $12,000,000 and this does not include the money spent by property owners and merchants on improving their plumbing, heating and electrical systems and the general upgrading of their facilities.

(iii) The Role of Financial Institutions

During the first years of Gastown's revival, financial institutions came into continued criticism for their lack of support. According to one writer, the "negative reception by financial institutions (became) infuriating". Consequently, much of the early recycling work was done with the entrepreneurs' own money.

After the financial success of recycling activity was firmly established, some lenders began to acquire interest in the area. Now loans appear available to entrepreneurs who have already proved themselves; but some still complain that interest rates are higher than on other construction projects.

(iv) The Role of Insurance Companies

According to the head of the Gastown Merchants Association, Gastown did not face a major problem of redlining (i.e. mass discrimination) by insurance companies. As long as the civic fire marshall considered the building fit for occupation, a fire insurance policy was available . . . at a price.

Theft insurance has been another story. Until last year, even the government's own insurance company had allegedly redlined the area for theft insurance. This practice now appears to have stopped, but theft insurance remains extremely expensive. It is unclear whether this attitude exists because insurance companies still believe the area to be a hippie haven (which it ceased to be long ago) or whether it reflects a lack of confidence in the adequacy of municipal police protection in the area. In either case, the cost is being borne by local proprietors. Fortunately, unlike fire insurance, it does not have a major impact upon the availability of mortgage financing.

EFFECTS UPON THE AREA

(i) Commercial Use

The transformation of Gastown's commercial character is made obvious by the following findings.

Many of the old low-intensity uses disappeared. The floor area occupied by wholesalers or left vacant in 1966 amounted to nearly 50 per cent of the total floor area in Gastown. In 1974, this figure had declined to 30 per cent. The floor area occupied by wholesalers decreased from 1,075,000 square feet to 780,000 square feet, a decrease of 27 per cent.

On the other hand, the floor area occupied by retail establishments increased by 200,000 square feet or 147 per cent between 1966 and 1974. The floor area occupied by restaurants and entertainment establishments more than doubled from 86,000 square feet to 178,000 square feet. The floor area occupied by offices increased from 280,000 square feet to 450,000 in 1974.

New "Gastown-compatible" retail/restaurant sales, which are directly related to the commercial rehabilitation activities in the historic area and which are vital to Gastown's revival and the area's economy, amounted to $17,720,000 in 1974. It is estimated that approximately 9 million dollars was accounted for by tourism.

Vacancy rates, although considerably higher when compared to other similar areas in the City, have declined by 50 per cent from 20% of the total floor area in 1966 to 10% in 1974. Furthermore, the outlook for vacant buildings is considerably different now than it was for many unoccupied structures in 1966: in 1966, it was difficult to find companies prepared to rent or lease floor space in these obsolete structures. Unoccupied buildings now tend to be concentrated on the eastern and western fringes of Gastown. The City Planning Department, however, expects many of these cases to be strictly a temporary situation, since many of these vacancies have resulted from the short-term effects of functional shifts from warehousing or storage uses to more intensive uses — offices and retail stores.

The retail market has seen noticeable change. The 1966 ground floor use pattern reflected the existence of functional obsolescence of the buildings in the area. A large number of buildings, especially around Maple Tree Square, had been struck by functional obsolescence; many had become completely unusable prior to 1966 and therefore more than 15 per cent of the total ground floor area stood vacant. Nearly 24 per cent of the ground floor area in Gastown, especially along Water Street and East and West Cordova Street was occupied by firms such as wholesalers and warehousing companies requiring low rental rates. Scattered throughout the area were corner grocery stores catering to the "Skid Road" resident.

Many warehouses have been converted to desirable office space such as this

By 1974, ground floor data suggested that extensive changes had taken place. Ninety "Gastown-compatible" retail stores and 33 "Gastown-compatible" restaurant/entertainment establishments were located in Gastown, many of them around Maple Tree Square, Water Street, and West Cordova. These retailers and restaurants have in general replaced "wholesale type" and "industrial-type" establishments or have taken over formerly vacant space. Of the total floor area occupied by "Gastown-compatible" retail establishments, 125,000 square feet (63% of the total) in 1974 was located on the ground floor, the rest on the second floor or in the basement.

When one also takes into consideration new non-retail uses, the following picture emerges. By 1974 (the last year for which figures are available), 150 new firms had established in Gastown. Some of these businesses have now spread worldwide; but within Gastown itself, they have generated an estimated $25,000,000 in annual sales and employ over 1,000 people.

(ii) Property Values

Property values can be expected to increase in accordance with the intensification of use.

The estimated overall market value of all properties in Gastown increased from 19.9 million dollars in 1966 to over 60 million dollars in 1974, an increase of 200 per cent.

Between 1965 and 1968, 43 property market transactions with a registered value of $4,146,925 occurred within the present boundaries of the Gastown Historic Site area. Of these 43 market transactions, 10 properties sold below their assessed value: 4 properties in 1965, 3 properties in 1966, 2 properties in 1967 and one in 1968. Some properties sold at up to 63 percent below their assessed value, with the majority of the other nine properties selling 10 per cent to 30 per cent below assessed value. Since 1969, no properties have been sold below their assessed value.

Building Permit Activity
in $1,000,000

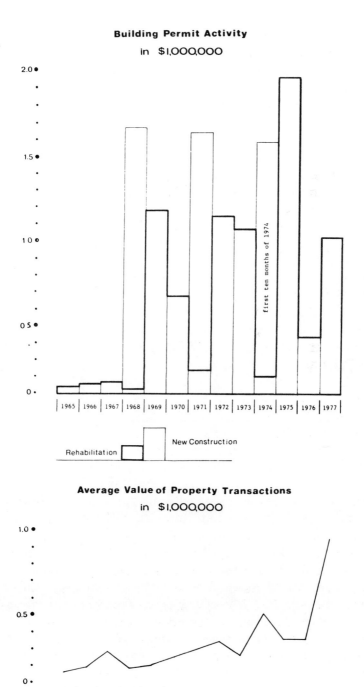

Rehabilitation
New Construction

first ten months of 1974

| 1965 | 1966 | 1967 | 1968 | 1969 | 1970 | 1971 | 1972 | 1973 | 1974 | 1975 | 1976 | 1977 |

Average Value of Property Transactions
in $1,000,000

| 1965 | 1966 | 1967 | 1968 | 1969 | 1970 | 1971 | 1972 | 1973 | 1974 | 1975 | 1976 | 1977 |

As more and more investors became aware of the long term potential of Gastown, demand for real estate in the area increased, forcing up real estate values throughout the area. These higher market values for properties excluded the admission of various types of enterprises — typically low rent users — and encouraged the property owners, in order to make a high return on their investments, to renovate their buildings and to rent them out to retailers and to other more intensive users.

The average value of a property transaction was around $29,000 in 1964; increased tourist business made property increasingly valuable. This resulted in an average market value increase from $55,325 in 1965 to about $156,275 in 1973, an increase of 182 per cent. Expressed in 1973 constant dollars, the real value increased from $78,900 in 1965 to $156,275 in 1973, still an increase of 98 per cent. A recent report from the City of Vancouver Planning Department placed the average value of a property market transaction in 1977 at $940,000.

RECOUPING THE PUBLIC INVESTMENT

(i) Introduction

Many of the objectives of urban renewal were accomplished without the usual expenses and delays associated with this process. A rundown, "Skid Road" type area was transformed without the lengthy planning process required for urban renewal, without public land acquisition, and without having to demolish the buildings, into a vibrant part of Vancouver's downtown area.

In addition, of course, a portion of history could be saved for future generations; and a milieu was created for Vancouverites which was so environmentally pleasing that its popularity exceeded all expectations. This phenomenon is discussed in the next section.

In short, a wide range of public purposes was achieved. This, in itself, should probably make the investment worthwhile. Many municipal politicians in

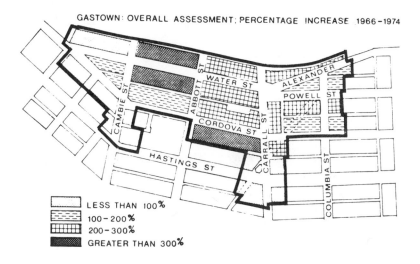

LESS THAN 100%
100-200%
200-300%
GREATER THAN 300%

Canada, however, do not think in those terms: unlike freeways and other such things, heritage areas must be shown to pay for themselves. Fortunately, Gastown passes the test in a most conclusive manner.

(ii) Increases in Property Assessment

As mentioned earlier, appraised value of property is the base on which municipal taxes are computed.

Overall assessment, which includes land and improvement assessment, rose by 147 per cent from $12,5700,000 in 1966 to $31,016,000 in 1974. (Expressed in 1966 *constant* dollars, this represents an increase in the overall assessment of more than 60 percent). This compares with a City-wide overall assessment increase (unadjusted) for commercial and industrial properties of 127 per cent. Property assessments have been frozen since 1974 pending provincial review of assessment policies.

Some interesting points materialize when individual blocks within the historic area are compared with each other. Blocks which so far have undergone partial or complete revitalization and commercial rehabilitation show an overall assessment increase of between 200 and 300 per cent, whereas the remaining blocks, which have

259

undergone little or no improvement, show an increase of between 20 and 80 per cent.

There are, of course, some extraneous reasons. One reason for the increase in the assessed value of Gastown property is the proximity of parts of Project 200 to Gastown and the potential of Vancouver's Harbour Waterfront, which could have been a major factor in the increased land assessment. It is also the result of the area's location adjacent to the Downtown Vancouver Business District.

However, rehabilitation of commercial structures seems to have been the major factor in the rapid increase of the assessed land and improvements in Gastown. For example, all structures in the blocks along Water Street, Cordova Street, Powell, Alexander and Carrall Streets, which underwent an intensive rehabilitation process and conversion activities to higher use, experienced improvement assessments of between 200 per cent and 500 per cent and in most cases, land assessment increased above 150 per cent between 1966 and 1974.

Despite these increases, there are still some officials who claim that Gastown is under-assessed. The implications of higher assessments which translate into increased property and business taxes are extensive. If assessments and taxes are raised, the impact on both the property owners and commercial institutions would be considerable. Although higher assessments would raise tax revenues to the City, higher taxes would also have the effect of forcing industrial and smaller commercial operations to leave Gastown and would increase the pressures to convert various structures to a higher more intensive use. In addition, many smaller businesses, which are vital in maintaining the character of the area, would be forced to leave Gastown because of higher rents.

(iii) Tax Revenues

In line with higher general purpose land and improvement assessments, general property taxes increased from $165,000 in 1966 to $536,000 in 1977, an increase of 223 per cent. Although these figures for 1966 and 1977 are not directly comparable because of changes in assessment procedures and changes in the rates of taxation, they do give a reasonably accurate indication that in terms of general taxes, the City has benefited from the rehabilitation activities in the Gastown Area.

VISITORS TO GASTOWN

(i) Introduction

Gastown was renovated primarily for money. Who are the visitors and shoppers who provide the economic life blood of the area? There are certainly a lot of them. According to the Vancouver City Planning Department, new "Gastown-compatible retail/restaurant sales" amounted to approximately $17.7 million in 1974. Total expenditure by an estimated 1.8 — 2 million tourists entering Gastown (of the more than 7 million tourists in Greater Vancouver in 1974 spending more than $500 million) amounted to approximately $9 million. It has been estimated that up to 25,000 people enter the historic area on a warm sunny day in the summer months.

To get a better idea of who these people are and how they spend their money, the Planning Department conducted a special survey in 1975. The following are the results.

(ii) Area of Origin of Visitors

Interviews revealed that at almost any given time, some 44 percent of visitors are from the Vancouver area, and some 56 percent are from out of town. This suggests that Gastown is a powerful tourist attraction, but is not exclusively so: the high proportion of Vancouverites indicates that the area is definitely an integral part of the community.

A larger percentage of Vancouverites visits the area during the noon hours and in the afternoon (20.7 percent and 22.1 percent of the total visitors) compared with 16.8 percent of the total during the evening hours. This is probably due to the fact that many Vancouverites

Gastown Pigeon Deterrent. Pigeons are Gastowns' only unwelcome visitors

visiting Gastown work in nearby commercial facilities and enter the Gastown area on shopping and luncheon trips. By comparison, a larger percentage of United States residents visit Gastown during the evening, 26.2 percent of the total visitors, compared with 20.2 percent of the total around noon and 21.5 percent of the total in the afternoon.

(iii) Reasons for Visiting Gastown

The most frequently mentioned reason for coming to Gastown is "window shopping" and "browsing". This is mentioned by more than 55 percent of all responding Gastown visitors. Many experts believe that this is simply another way of saying that visitors come to enjoy the atmosphere of the area. A smaller percentage of City residents mention this reason (41 percent) compared with suburbanites (54 percent) and tourists (63 percent). The high response of tourists is predictable; however, the high response of suburbanites can perhaps be interpreted as a comment on the "atmosphere" (or lack of it) in the typical Canadian suburb.

The next most frequently mentioned reason is "shopping" with 30 percent. This figure automatically distinguishes Gastown from the typical retail area or shopping

Place of Origin	Time Period 10AM — 10PM
	%
Gastown	2.8
Downtown Vancouver	4.2
City of Vancouver	20.2
Metro Vancouver	17.1
Lower Mainland	3.4
Rest of BC	6.9
Rest of Canada	17.4
United States	22.3
Other Countries	5.6
	100.0

mall, where the comparable figure would probably be close to 100 percent. It is consequentially no coincidence that many retailers are oriented to either "speciality" shops or "impulse" buying.

"To eat and to drink" ranks as the next important reason for visiting Gastown. This is mentioned by nearly 29 percent of all Gastown visitors. It is more often mentioned by suburbanites with 34 percent and tourists with 31 percent. By comparison only 21 percent of City of Vancouver residents mention this reason; again, this is perhaps a tacit comment on the typical suburb. Only 2 percent of all Gastown visitors mention "entertainment" as a reason for visiting Gastown; this is puzzling when one considers that there are at least 10 night clubs in the historic area catering to visitors at night.

(iv) The Visitors' Verdict — Pros and Cons

Is Gastown a success in the eyes of visitors? This is a question which is partly answered by the economic and commercial results outlined earlier; however, the *Gastown Visitors' Survey* unearthed further information concerning the assets and liabilities of the renovated area.

The most frequently stated aspect of the character of Gastown enjoyed by visitors is the "variety of unique shops". This is mentioned by nearly 32 percent of all responding people. The next most enjoyed feature is the "atmosphere" with nearly 26 percent, followed by "the little yards, squares and beautified streets" with more than 16 percent. "People" and "walking around" rank together as fourth and fifth with 14 percent. Next, "restaurants" and "architecture of buildings" rank nearly together with 10.5 percent and 10 percent.

When asked what they do not like about Gastown, "traffic problems" and "social problems" (drunks, panhandlers) are the most frequently mentioned "dislikes". "Traffic problems" is mentioned by nearly 14 percent out of all persons responding and social problems by more than 10 percent. "Parking problems" is next with 6.3 percent followed by "construction on Water Street" with 5.6 percent; this had not been completed at the time of the survey. "Shops and merchants are too expensive" was next with 5.4 percent followed by "too commercialized" with 4.8 percent and "tourist trap" with 2.8 percent of all persons responding.

(v) Reason for Visit — Knowledge of Gastown

A remarkable 73 percent of all Gastown visitors from the Metro Vancouver area come to Downtown Vancouver in the summer months *because of Gastown*. More than 67 percent of all tourists have at least a general idea of the Gastown area before coming to Vancouver. 58 percent of those tourists having an advance knowledge of Gastown

264

before coming to Vancouver know it through friends, 11 percent through radio and television, 16 percent through a tourist brochure and 12 percent through newspapers and magazines. This predominance of word-of-mouth is significant: first, it shows that Gastown leaves a lasting impression. Second, it is a sobering reminder to businessmen and officials who think that tourism budgets should be devoted to advertising without regard to the product advertised. The Gastown experience shows that if one offers an interesting product, much of the publicity will take care of itself.

More than 10 percent of all tourists feel that the presence of Gastown affects the total amount of time spent in Vancouver. They mention that they spend between 1 hour and 1 day longer in Vancouver because of the presence of Gastown.

(vi) Number of Visits - Metro Vancouverites

More than 31 percent of all Metro Vancouverites visiting, passing through, or on business in Gastown had been in the historic area twenty or more times between August 1974 and July 1975. 13 percent had been in Gastown between six and ten times, 13.5 percent twice and nearly 12 percent five times. Only 10 percent had never been in Gastown before. This would suggest that Gastown is a continuing attraction, enjoying "repeat business".

(vii) Comparison of Gastown with other Historic Areas

When comparing Gastown with other historic areas in North America (Pioneer Square, Seattle; Old Montreal; Bastion Square, Victoria) nearly 87 percent of all responding people feel that Gastown is larger in size than other historic areas they have visited. 79 percent feel that prices are lower, 73 percent find a larger variety of activities in Gastown and 67 percent find more atmosphere there. On the negative side, a staggering 87 percent feel that other historic areas in North America are more "authentic". This raises a multitude of ques-

AVERAGE MONEY EXPENDITURES
OF METRO VANCOUVERITES AND TOURISTS
FOR THREE TIME PERIODS, 1975

	Weighted Average Expenditures All Items	Average Expenditures Restaurants	Average Expenditures All Merchandise
Metro Vancouverites 10am—2pm	$7.06	$3.47	$11.95
Tourists	$6.85	$4.31	$9.95
Metro Vancouverites 2pm—6pm	$5.98	$4.35	$7.86
Tourists	$5.81	$4.51	$7.67
Metro Vancouverites 6pm—10pm	$5.81	$5.59	$6.39
Tourists	$6.13	$5.18	$8.47

tions. Has Gastown's festive atmosphere been overdone? Or is this widespread conclusion due to ignorance of the fact that Gastown's original atmosphere was even rowdier than the status quo? Whatever the answer, these misgivings appear to be no obstacle to public support and enjoyment of the area.

(viii) Spending

Gastown exhibits a very interesting paradox: despite the fact that a majority of visitors enter the area without the intention of spending money, more than 60 percent of the total purchase merchandise or eat in Gastown.

Average money expenditure per person per visit was $6.22 during the summer months of 1975; the average amount of money spent in restaurants amounted to $4.73 for the period between 10 AM and 10 PM, and total average expenditure for all merchandise items was $8.72.

(xi) Summary

The general impression which one receives from the above data is that although approximately 25 percent of all tourists entering Greater Vancouver visit the historic Gastown area, they spend just over 1 percent of the total tourist dollar spent in Greater Vancouver. This is largely because tourist hotels, which absorb a large part of tourist expenditure, are not located in Gastown. Nevertheless, the City Planning Department has concluded that it does not appear that Gastown yet plays "an important role" in influencing visitors to come to the Vancouver area as there are many other tourist attractions in the Vancouver area. However, the fact that Gastown provokes a longer stay in Vancouver presumably has an indirect positive effect on total tourist spending.

The variety of shops and the unique atmosphere of the area appear to be the major attraction of Gastown. These retail outlets receive more than 53% of the total tourist dollar spent in Gastown against 47% for restaurants and entertainment establishments in 1974. The beautified streets, people watching, browsing around and the architecture of the buildings are also enjoyed by visitors and Vancouverites. The unique character of the area preserved through historic designation and capital improvement projects not only provides an attraction but creates an environment which results in more economic activities like "Gastown — compatible" shops and restaurants.

A solution to the traffic and parking problem during the summer months, improvements in regard to the social problems and washroom facilities are high on the list of improvements suggested, not only by visitors but by the business community of the area. Frequently, it is mentioned that Gastown should be open to all income groups in terms of merchandise offered and restaurant facilities. Fear is expressed that Gastown might become too commercial, or a tourist trap. It is therefore suggested that city police and merchants' attitudes should be more closely geared to the preservation of the informal and unique character of the area.

ECONOMIC FLUCTUATION

The unusual character of Gastown creates certain inherent economic tendencies which should be noted.

The visitors' survey proved that the majority of visitors come to browse, not to shop. This feature makes Gastown's retail function fundamentally different from that of the typical retail centre: a much higher percentage of purchases are due to impulse in Gastown than in other areas.

A major exception to "impulse" buying in Gastown is the purchase of "specialty" items or "luxury" items (e.g. in art galleries). Furthermore, Gastown's restaurants and bars are a major attraction.

The combination of these four major marketing objects ("impulse" items, "specialty" items, "luxury" items and "entertainment") make Gastown unusually subject to economic fluctuations. During times of economic growth, Gastown can be expected to boom at a considerably higher rate than the economy as a whole, since people have more money to spend on precisely what Gastown provides. Inversely, during times of economic contraction Gastown can be expected to suffer far more than the economy as a whole.

This phenomenon of accelerated fluctuation has been seen in other heritage districts in Canada, e.g. Old Montreal. Gastown, however, has a partly stabilizing factor which Old Montreal does not: whereas most Old Montreal buildings rely *exclusively* on ground floor retail for income (leaving upper floors underutilized), Gastown has recycled a higher proportion of upper floors for office space, which is not as prone to fluctuations.

Another heritage district, Old Quebec, has an even more stabilizing factor: it has a large residential population. Unfortunately, few measures are being taken to prevent the displacement of that population by "entertainment-oriented" uses, and consequently the area is likely to encounter more extreme economic fluctuation in the future than it does now.

Gastown has almost no residential population. If it did, this would probably have a stabilizing influence upon the fluctuations of retail trade in the area. Increased office use of above-ground space would also be helpful. It is only by matching retail use of ground-floor space with effective non-retail use of above-ground floor space that the boom-or-bust character of the area can be mitigated.

FURTHER ECONOMIC IMPLICATIONS

Some economic implications of the Gastown experience are impossible to quantify. One is the spirit of entrepreneurship, described by Mr. Ed Keate, President of the Downtown Businessmen's Association:

> *It would be nice to say that Gastown means "X" dollars to Vancouver but, as one of the minor players in the piece, I cannot honestly attach a dollar figure. What I can attach is a knowledge that Gastown has put a lot of woof in the warp and woof of Vancouver's social fabric. It would be impossible to measure Gastown's allure as a tourist or convention attraction.*
>
> *Unlike many other North American cities where going out at night can be unsafe or risky, Gastown is a haven for some of Vancouver's better restaurants and shops. Of greater significance is the fact that a former liability is now being openly touted for the genuine attraction that it is.*

But the Gastown transformation also fostered a spirit of entrepreneurship that has reverberated throughout the community. Other business and ethnic areas within Vancouver's boundaries have observed the Gastown success and have sought as much or more for their own. It is the domino effect, with one improvement feeding upon the next.

City Hall can tell you that in return for their beautification investment of $1 million they now have on the tax rolls Gastown properties with a total assessment increase of $18.5 million, and from that added assessed value they will extract, in 1977 alone, approximately one-third million in additional property taxes. But that does not tell you that a company that got its start in Gastown (and still has its head office there) now generates millions elsewhere, nor does it tell you of the ideas and concepts that were nurtured in Gastown and now flourish elsewhere.

Whether Gastown succeeds in increasing business by 10% or 110% within the next decade is really academic. Entrepreneurs who got their business starts in Gastown have subsequently spread their talents and abilities to other parts of Vancouver, Canada, North America and the World.

CHAPTER 18

SOME PRELIMINARY CONCLUSIONS

This case study has been simply an overview of Gastown, just as this entire text has been an overview of Canadian conservation techniques. It has touched upon some of the salient points; but it has not studied causal relationships. It is hoped that an in-depth study can follow at a future date.

Within that limited context, however, certain preliminary conclusions can nevertheless be drawn concerning the nature and practice of heritage conservation not only in Gastown, but also in Canada as a whole.

Earlier in this text, it was mentioned that the Canadian heritage movement is a coalition. Vancouver is a perfect example. The motives of the merchants, the historians, the culture fans, and the neighbouring Chinese community were all different, but these groups nevertheless worked successfully together. Gastown also exemplifies the importance of the economic and social rationale for conservation; these arguments were as basic to the citizens' movement as any pure "heritage" considerations.

It was also stated at the beginning of this text that "the very existence of the organized movement is remarkable when one understands the forces which were militating against it". These forces were evident enough in Gastown, and underlined the unfortunate adversarial nature which so often besets heritage conservation efforts in this country.

Vancouver also epitomizes the way in which so many misconceptions prevail in the Canadian municipal descision-making process. Every social, economic and ideological myth was invoked to denounce the conservationists as lunatics or as anti-capitalist reactionaries (a new breed of subversive invented for the occasion). This treatment is repeated in many communities throughout the country . . . until these communities take the effort to study conservation seriously.

This is the achievement of the City of Vancouver: it was finally persuaded to study conservation with an open mind . . . even though it took ten years for citizens to persuade it to do so. When it looked seriously at the possibilities, the City reversed its anti-heritage policy. Smaller men and women would not have had the largesse to admit such a reversal of policy; this is to Vancouver's enduring credit.

The fact nevertheless remains that citizen action was undoubtedly indispensable to the achievement of this objective.

There will always be a need for citizen action . . . if only to find out what government is doing. The struggle for Gastown epitomized the problems which undue governmental secrecy can lead to. This dilemma invariably leads to tensions between non-governmental organizations and government; for officials often assume that the existence of a citizen's group is a direct reflection upon their own performance. Subconsciously, it is probable that the very creation of citizens' groups is viewed by many Canadian officials as tacit criticism. Every time conservationists open their mouths, the situation only gets worse.

Conservationists in Canada are therefore faced with a seemingly eternal problem of balancing their comments so that they provoke governmental action without precipitating a breakdown of essential communications. Some Canadian conservationists have chosen to work hand-in-glove with officials . . . and have thus made themselves invisible. In Gastown, on the other hand, conservationists did not hesitate to denounce some government proposals, and to do so vehemently. They got away with it for three main reasons:

a) they had good credibility (particularly their businessmen);

b) Some of the conservationists were acting out of purely altruistic motives, whereas others "put their money where their mouth is" by investing in the area; and, most importantly,

c) they had well-organized and highly visible popular support, as well as a flair for promotion.

In a political context, the last element can be decisive. Like many battles, however, the struggle for Gastown was won also with the help of a little luck and an enormous amount of intestinal fortitude.

On the other hand, most battles have many losers and few winners; Gastown is the reverse. Despite incredible odds, it was created in such a way that its economic benefits to the community became as obvious as its social and cultural benefits. Since the Gastown experience, conservationists can make their voices heard with more confidence than ever before.

There is another aspect of Gastown which strikes a more personal note: it is the very real sense in which many people who worked on behalf of Gastown identified with the early pioneers.

As mentioned earlier, there was a merchant who commented on the occasion when bureaucrats forced Gassy Jack Deighton's saloon to be relocated. "Gastown was moved once"; he said, "it will not be moved again". It became very obvious that, as far as the speaker was concerned, this phrase was more than rhetoric: it reflected a sincere belief that the people responsible for Gastown's revival were the spiritual heirs of that weird bunch of characters who built the community in the first place.

On this point, it is interesting to note something which the Merchant's Association did, not in Gastown, but rather some twenty miles away in New Westminster with relatively less publicity. It placed a new headstone at the grave of Gassy Jack Deighton. That gesture was revealing of a feature which is fundamental to Gastown.

Broadcaster Gary Bannerman put the matter most honestly and concisely:

> The new Gastown is the same as the original community. It never was much of a town. It was simply a spirit!

Respect for the initiative of the past is the inspiration for the initiative of the future: that hypothesis was proposed by Majorian to the Romans. Canadians can no longer treat it solely as an hypothesis: 1500 years later and half a globe away, its truth is now being demonstrated.

Is this the kind of future which is in store for the heritage of Canada?

The answer to that question is not a simple one. In order to make our heritage a positive force in the future evolution of our society, then the mechanics of our society must be geared accordingly. The threat to our architectural and historic environment has not arisen by accident: it was *built into* the legal, financial and fiscal arrangements which quietly direct Canadian patterns of development. Until changes are made in those institutional structures, the menace to our architectural past will keep inevitably recurring in various communities across Canada.

This book has outlined some of the areas which must be dealt with. Heritage conservation must first be regarded in an interdisciplinary way: its rationale lies not only in history and architecture, but also in sociology, social psychology, and economics. These are all subjects in which research relating to conservation is barely beginning, and which deserve further attention.

Even the historical and architectural dimensions of heritage are frequently misunderstood. The common denominator of all heritage worthy of conservation is *achievement*; it is in that context, and not in a rigidly formalistic analysis of history or architecture, that

274

authorities and conservationists must approach the task of defining the heritage which Canada seeks to protect.

Further legislative improvements are required at all levels. Attention should be paid to the obligations of the federal government and other governments regarding the heritage property which they own themselves; the creation of bodies such as the FACCHC is an encouraging sign of things to come. Heritage legislation at the provincial and municipal levels is also filled with loopholes; but steady progress is being made, and conservationists must endeavour to keep the momentum alive.

Unfortunately, even a good law is not worth the paper it's written on unless it is enforced. This problem is likely to face conservationists for years to come. Their task would be much easier, however, if the fundamentally unfair laws respecting citizens' groups were changed. If indeed governments are committed to public participation and citizens' rights, then no effort should be spared in tackling problems such as *locus standi*, access to information, the right to political activity etc.

Finally, it is essential to obtain a better economic deal for the conservation and renovation of heritage. Increasing attention should of course be paid to subsidy programs; but even more important is the question of the tax treatment of heritage property. The current system of subsidizing demolition without encouraging renovation is unacceptable and must be reversed if a comprehensive program of conservation ever wishes to be economically realistic.

The scope of the task ahead sometimes appears intimidating; but it should not be a deterrent. Never before in Canadian history have so many citizens across this country joined together for the protection of our built environment; and never before have so many sympathizers found their way into the nooks and crannies of the power structure. Despite all the ups and downs which Canadian citizens' groups have endured from bureaucracy, at no time in our history have we had as many enlightened and conscientious officials discreetly seeking ways to improve the context for heritage conservation. At long last citizens are beginning to feel that government is no longer the brick wall it once was.

Conservationists have succeeded in isolating the major problems which require attention; that is already a giant leap forward. Many tentative solutions have been formulated; it is now largely a question of putting them into practice. Conservationists have even done the seemingly impossible: in one case, they have taken an area and, despite the most adverse conditions possible (including riots, dilapidation, opposition from every level of government etc.) turned the area into the vibrant district which Gastown is today. If the conservation movement is capable of that degree of creativity even when handcuffed by the legislative *status quo,* then the mind boggles at the possibilities which would be attainable in a reformed legal, financial and fiscal context.

If the current momentum for change can be maintained, then that context might be within our grasp within the next decade. The one element which, above all else, is indispensable to that momentum is the element which Gary Bannerman described as the essence of Gastown: "spirit."

This may seem like a curious place to launch into a definition of a "conservationist"; after all, this book has referred to this strange creature continuously. But "better late than never"; and indeed, the definition is quite simple: it has only two ingredients.

First, a conservationist is a person who hopes that his surroundings will improve, not only through the elimination of less desirable elements, but also by conserving and promoting the better aspects of those surroundings. Second, a conservationist is a person who feels sufficiently part of those surroundings that he or she is prepared to work with fellow citizens so that such improvement can come about.

Tens of thousands of Canadians correspond to that definition; but for every active participant of a conservationist organization, there are a hundred Canadians who sympathize but who fail to take part because they lack the time or because they labour under the miscon-

"To communicate is the beginning of understanding"

ception that heritage conservation, however nice, won't work. This book has shown that heritage can work for us . . . if we give it the right tools.

Those tools include law, finance, tax policy and promotion; but the most important is public support. Public support is the pivot on which all other movement for reform is based.

Certainly it is time for all Canadians to consider the future of their built environment, and to co-operate for the protection of the qualities which that environment embodies. This Canadian heritage can be given the place it deserves; but, John Milton notwithstanding, they do *not* also serve who only stand and wait.

PHOTO CREDITS

Front Cover André Ellefsen.
Page 3 Canadian Government Office of Tourism.
Page 20 Heritage Canada.
Page 23 Frank Chalmers.
Page 24 Top and right, City of Montreal Housing and Planning Department.
Bottom, Ontario Ministry of Housing.
Page 26 Top, Kryn Taconis, N.F.B. Photothèque.
Bottom, Les éditions de l'homme.
Page 27 Watson-Guptill publications.
Page 29 Right, United Way of Greater Vancouver.
Below, Heritage Canada.
Page 30 Chateau Developments, Edmonton.
Page 33 Montreal Star-Canada Wide.
Inset, Sauvons Montréal.
Page 37 Top and bottom, Royal Ontario Museum.
Page 40 Von Matt and Kuhner, Librarie Hachette.
Page 41 Heritage Canada and Newfoundland Historic Trust.
Page 43 Top, Canadian Government Office of Tourism.
Bottom, National Maritime Museum London, loan from Ministry of Defense-Navy.
Page 44 James Knight.
Page 45 Provincial Archives of Alberta.
Page 46 Left and right, Canadian Government Office of Tourism.
Page 47 Canadian Government Office of Tourism.
Page 48 Canadian Government Office of Tourism.
Page 49 Marc Denhez.
Page 51 Top, Canadian Government Office of Tourism.
Bottom, Macdonald Stewart Foundation.
Page 52 Michael Semak, National Film Board.
Page 53 Canadian Government Office of Tourism.
Page 54 Top, Heritage Canada.
Bottom, Canadian Government Office of Tourism.
Page 55 Clockwise, from top left: Canadian Government Office of Tourism, Canadian Government Office of Tourism, Wally Stewart and Heritage Canada.
Page 56 Clockwise, from top left, Marc Denhez, Canadian Inventory of Historic Building, Jay Coulter, Saskatchewan Department of Culture and Recreation, Toronto Globe and Mail.
Page 57 Vancouver Public Library.
Inset, Canadian Imperial Bank of Commerce.
Page 58 Marc Denhez.
Page 59 Canadian Government Office of Tourism.
Page 60 Geological Survey of Canada.
Page 61 Department of Northern Saskatchewan.
Page 62 Public Archives of Canada.
Page 65 Top, Manitoba Archives.
Bottom, Bary Downs.
Page 70 Marc Denhez.

278

Page 71   Left, Public Archives of Canada.
           Right, Heritage Canada.
Page 72   Garth Pritchard, The Gazette.
Page 79   Left, Air Canada.
           Right, Canadian Government Office of Tourism.
Page 83   Canadian Inventory or Historic Building.
Page 86   Top, Newfoundland Historic Trust.
           Bottom, Jim Cochrane.
Page 89   Department of Indian Affairs and Northern Development.
Page 96   Canadian Inventory of Historic Building.
Page 99   The Toronto Star.
Page 112   Wally Stewart.
Page 113   Above, Public Archives of Prince Edward Island.
           Below, P.E.I. Heritage Foundation.
Page 114   Top, Marcelle Jubinville.
           Bottom, John Leaning.
Page 115   Ken Kelly.
Page 118   Left, Public Archives of Manitoba. Right, Heritage Canada.
Page 132   Lunenburg Heritage Society.
Page 134   James Knight.
Page 143   Guy & Normand Roy.
Page 146   René Magritte, The Castle of the Pyrenees, 1959 (Private Collection
           New York) © A.D.A.G.P.
Page 147   Heritage Canada.
Page 152   Roy Peterson.
Page 156   Peter Lynde, U.B.C. Alumni Chronicle.
Page 161   Top, Norris, The Vancouver Sun.
           Bottom, Vancouver Sun.
Page 168   Top Carleton County Historical Society.
           Bottom, Langham Cultural Society.
Page 170   Heritage Canada.
Page 173   Clockwise from top left, Armand Legault, Canadian Press; Margaret
           Lewis; Murray Bradley; Margaret Lewis.
Page 179   Montreal Gazette.
Page 184   Vancouver City Archives.
Page 185   Vancouver Public Library.
Page 186   Vancouver City Archives.
Page 188   Vancouver Sun.
Page 190   Top, City of Vancouver Planning Department.
           Bottom, Heritage Canada.
Page 191   Vancouver Province.
Page 194   Myfawny Phillips.
Page 195   Vancouver Sun.
Page 198   Project 200 Properties Limited.
Page 199   Heritage Canada.
Page 204   Vancouver Sun.
Page 205   Larry Killam, Lagoon Estates Ltd.
Page 210   Marathon Realty.
Page 227   Marc Denhez.
Page 235   Franco Citarella.

INDEX

Meaning of "Heritage" (intro) (p. 40)

Tone - sarcasm / immature humour (44)

Purpose? ① general primer
② treatise on law
③ case study

Polarization - Conservationist
H. Movement
- Battle analogy - title
- Confrontationist
- General personalization - "they"
do this + that ...

subheadings - textbook -